£4.50 TRA

32/23 MATT

Non fiction Gift Aid
£

40 000650

D0590313

Extraordinary VILLAGES

Dungeness

Extraordinary VILLAGES

Tony Francis

Merlin Unwin Books

First published in Great Britain by Merlin Unwin Books, 2014

Text © Tony Francis

Photographs © individual photographers (see pages 223-4)

All rights reserved, including the right to reproduce this book or portions thereof in any form or by any means, electronic or mechanical, including photocopying, recording, or by any information storage and retrieval system, without permission in writing from the publisher. All inquiries should be addressed to:

Merlin Unwin Books Ltd

Palmers House, 7 Corve Street, Ludlow, Shropshire SY8 1DB

www.merlinunwin.co.uk

The author asserts his moral right to be identified with this work.

Designed and set in Minion Pro by Merlin Unwin

Printed by Great Wall Printing in Hong Kong

ISBN 978 1 906122 67 6

To Monica
who rode shotgun on a
number of my trips

CONTENTS

The Publishers would like to thank all the photographers who have contributed to this book. Full photo credits on page 223.

INTRODUCTION

I hope this book will surprise and inspire you. It aims to capture the quirkiness of rural England and Wales and send readers on a different voyage of discovery. You'll find out which illustrious village has more false windows than any other and who put the snails in Snailbeach. If each chapter makes you say: 'Wow, I never realised that!', I've done my job.

I wanted to find out what it's like living on Lindisfarne where the tides control your day. I was curious to know whether villagers in the shadow of Europe's most gigantic coal-fired power station at Drax even noticed it any more. At the other end of the scale, the dreamy Cotswold parish of Great Tew, rescued from dereliction by the new lord of the manor is run as a commercial enterprise. Is this the way forward?

Having handpicked 50 villages with extraordinary tales to tell, I set off with my notebook and camera one snowy morning in April not knowing quite what to expect. What a fine adventure it turned out to be. I did most of the journeys by train – or to be precise, train and bus plus dozens of miles on foot.

It was an excellent way to get up close and personal with Britain, even though public transport once left me stranded on a deserted Cumbrian platform with no way of knowing why the scheduled service hadn't turned up, or whether it ever would. Freight trains carrying nuclear waste to Sellafield thundered past as darkness fell on this forsaken outpost.

It was all in the line of duty. Eventually a passenger train did arrive, though far too late for my connection home. Hearing my plight, the train operators paid for my bed and breakfast at Carlisle's finest hotel and got me home refreshed the following day. Thanks fellas.

There were many memorable moments. Like meeting Kathy Bartle in the last house standing on the crumbling cliffs of Aldbrough. Another 37 metres of erosion and it too will have to be evacuated. Kathy was remarkably sanguine. 'It's a lovely view,' she said.

Then there was the day I fell into a 1960s time-warp on Eel Pie Island and bumped into its most famous resident, Trevor Baylis, inventor of the wind-up radio.

And who could forget discovering Helmand Province in the middle of Norfolk? A small community of Afghans ran their stalls and tended their animals. Goat curry smelled deliciously incongruous. The call to prayer mingled with an exultation of skylarks.

You might wonder how I selected the villages for this exclusive club. I knew some of them from filming days on my TV programme Heart of the Country. Others were the result of painstaking research. Sometimes you only have to look at a map. Contours, population patterns and the shape of the coast speak volumes. My old geography teacher taught me that. Map reading was an important skill.

Why, for instance was there a village called Purton on both sides of the river Severn? What was the significance of a large, unpopulated area of East Anglia with no roads or markings of any sort? Were my eyes deceiving me or was there really a place called Sunk Island north of the Humber estuary? I had to find out. As you'll read, the answers are extraordinary.

A word of warning - two of the communities in this book aren't strictly speaking, villages. Winchelsea is supposed to be a town, though it has no political power. Its urbanity is a historical fluke. The mayor is a charming decoration. By contrast, Eel Pie Island is 'fifty drunks clinging to a rock', according to the folk who live there.

So what's the definition of a village? Normally it has a parish church, a parish council and a village sign at both ends. But in my book, a small group of people who take responsibility for their community and have a strong sense of place, also qualify for village status. So, welcome Eel Pie Island and don't be offended, Winchelsea.

Tony Francis
June 2014

Extraordinarily lucky: the village of Upper Slaughter (see page 184).

TERRA NON FIRMA

Aldbrough, East Yorkshire

Kathy Bartle was proud of her address. Cedar Cottage, Seaside Road, had a ring to it. She and her husband bought the cottage as a holiday home before deciding to move in permanently in 1988. The air was sweet. The wind was bracing. It made a refreshing change from Sheffield where noisy neighbours forced the couple to watch television in the garden shed – and eventually drove them out of town.

In the early days when Aldbrough was twice the village it is today, Seaside Road led to a T-junction and a coast road running parallel to the sea. There, a pub and a number of cliff-top cottages enjoyed fabulous views. They've all gone – victims of the North Sea which undermines soft boulder clay at the base of the cliffs and brings the top crashing down.

Today, 28 years after Kathy moved into her bijou bungalow, it stands on the precipice. A mere 37 metres of so-called terra firma separate Cedar Cottage from the deep. Seaside Road plunges off the edge of the world. A jagged line marks its sudden demise; a heap of crumbled tarmac, complete with fractured double yellow lines, leads down to the beach. Even the traffic wardens have given up. They figure nobody's going to park a car at 45 degrees! As for the original coast road – Kathy (74) and her husband Alan (81) are among the few who remember it. They also remember an amusement arcade, a café, a car park and a toilet block – all claimed by the sea. Welcome to Yorkshire's disappearing shoreline. Land at Aldbrough is being eroded at the rate of 1.8 metres a year. That's the height of the average man. It's a faster rate than anywhere else in Europe. The tidal drift is carrying chunks of the village in a southerly direction and dumping it either at Spurn Head or in Holland. Although Yorkshire folk are brought up to believe that the land slopes away from their beloved county, this is profoundly hurtful. Climate change and rising sea levels only spell further trouble.

East Riding Council keeps asking for a national fund to shore up Aldbrough's sea defences but nobody listens. What makes it all the more infuriating is that the neighbouring resorts of Mappleton and Withernsea *have* been protected. Mind you, the rest of this attractive village is on higher ground, three-quarters of a mile back from the cliffs and considers itself immune. I'd go so far as to say it's a split village. Us and Them. The sane and the insane. Period four-bedroom houses near the centre still fetch £400,000 plus. People work, drink, play football and sing hymns like villagers anywhere else. The fact that St. Bartholomew's church, the pubs, the chip shop and the Londis Stores are daily edging closer to the sea is met with a shrug of the shoulders, as if to say 'Yeah, yeah.'

At the sharp end of Aldbrough, visitors still flock to the caravan park even though some of the vans have been moved back from the brink, leaving empty hard-standings to tell their own story. Then there's the *Double Dutch* public house, whose demolish-by date must only be twelve years away. Apparently it's still doing business, although it looked quiet and forlorn to me. I met a middle-aged couple who walk the cliffs most days of the week, as if to keep a regular eye on the geology. The husband admitted:

'It feels as though the ground's slipping away under our feet', before adding: – 'But isn't it a beautiful spot?'

It certainly is. Despite the obvious danger of collapsing rock – and warnings about unexploded shells on the beach which 'could kill you' – members of the Aldbrough Fishing Club clamber down the cliff face to catch cod, skate, plaice and bass. Billy Hoe comes from Hull to fill his freezer, but it can be a dicey business.

'Some of the guys dig themselves into the bank and stand in water. You're risking your life even if you're only ankle deep. All it takes is one big wave.'

Billy remembers when Kathy's bungalow was more than a mile inland, not 37 metres as it is now. Needless to say, fishermen don't have the universal backing of coastal dwellers who accuse them of making things worse by digging into the rocks.

On the face of it, things couldn't get much worse for Kathy and Alan. They've been given another 8-10 years before they too must evacuate. As soon as the cliff edge gets to within eleven metres of a property, the council's obliged to pull it down. Previous evacuees have been rehoused in council homes or private rental properties, had their demolition and removal costs met and, in the case of private tenants, been reimbursed six months' rent. However, according to Jennifer Kippax, coastal officer for East Riding Council, the original £1.5m grant to cover all of that is running low and won't be replenished. So what support will there be for the Bartles? And what sense did it make to buy a house in the doomed part of Aldbrough in the first place? Erosion's not a new phenomenon after all. A staggering two and a half miles of Aldbrough has been lost since the Romans were here. Jennifer replied:

'Some people thought it was worth investing in a holiday area by the sea.'

Economic suicide though? She didn't disagree. The Bartles know they'll lose everything. That means the purchase price of £17,000 (and what it might have swollen to by now) as well as £11,000 spent on double-

Above left: This end of Aldbrough is relatively safe. However, a pub, an amusement arcade and several cottages have already disappeared from the other end.

glazing and a new roof. Are they off their trolley?

'No, we're okay,' Kathy reassured me. 'Our daughter's well placed, so inheritance isn't an issue. Cedar Cottage might last longer than us anyway.'

In the meantime, the couple battle against the odds to keep an attractive garden. Sea winds make it impossible to grow flowers and salt spray has killed the shrubs on the maritime side of the bungalow. They're also plagued by fishermen who clog up Seaside Road with their cars and equipment. Life on a cliff edge seems to fall some way short of Paradise. I put it to Kathy that there must be an upside to living in such an exposed place, otherwise she wouldn't have moved from Sheffield? She thought hard:

'That's a good question. At least we can *see* the sea now it's closer. And we haven't got next door neighbours!'

Below: The last house standing. Evacuation is imminent and unavoidable.

SEASIDE SPECTACULAR
Arnside, Cumbria

Close to midnight, under a full moon, Tim Cross waited beside the railway viaduct for the tide to come in. He was tense. His border terrier, Flick, sniffed agitatedly at the wet sand. A ten-metre bore was heading their way, one of the biggest of the year. In the distance, the moonlight added a touch of phosphor to the rising edge of wave. Tim wasn't alone. Hundreds of visitors had poured off the train to witness nature's sound and light show. Most of them were gathered at the end of the pier, an ideal vantage point.

Arnside has grown up at the confluence of four rivers which empty into the northernmost part of Morecambe Bay. When the tide sweeps in 'at the speed of a galloping horse', seawater pushes river water back in dramatic style. A coastguard called Colin Berry sounds the siren twice a day between March and October. You'll see him at the coastguard station wearing ear muffs to deaden the roar, and with binoculars trained on the distant swell. The first siren means 'get off the sands'. The second means 'Get off the sands *fast!*'

Back at the viaduct, Tim Cross was about to experience something special. I'll let him take up the story:

'I felt the pressure building up inside. My muscles tightened and my breathing got faster. It was a bit disconcerting. Then a thirty feet wall of water came thundering under the arches. It might have been thundering through my body. I'd never experienced anything like it. As soon as the waves passed, I felt relaxed again. As if someone had lifted a huge responsibility off my shoulders. The relief was tremendous. That's the power of the sea.'

Left: Arnside's famous railway viaduct offers great views of the tidal estuary.

Tim should know. He worked for Her Majesty's Coastguard Service for 25 years, rescuing walkers who ignored the sirens. Arnside's quicksand conceals many secrets. People, horses, even sheep have been sucked under. Across the Kent estuary at Cartmel Priory, there's a list of people who've vanished and a cemetery of unmarked graves. Morecambe Bay is one of the most dangerous sea areas in Britain.

All of which might put you off Arnside. It shouldn't. Its twice-daily tides are a constant source of entertainment. The sirens bring a shiver of excitement, an audio version of curtain-up. I sat on the terrace of Lesley Hornsby's award-winning guesthouse, No. 43, watching one of the gentler tides flood the bay. It measured only seven metres but was still impressive. Beached boats were suddenly bobbing about and seagulls swooped and dived as they followed the waves. The evening sun bathed everything in a soft orange. Lesley said:

'I never tire of this. Every tide is different. I have more photographs than I know what to do with!'

Across the estuary, someone else is studying the patterns of the sand. He has to. They change constantly. Yesterday's safe zone is today's hazard and vice versa. Cedric Robinson has been looking through his binoculars for half a century since he was appointed Her Majesty's Official Sandwalker. Cedric's 81 now but still a major player in these parts. He leads thousands of men, women, children and dogs on six-hour expeditions across this potentially treacherous landscape.

The group traditionally sets off from Arnside pier, wades the river Kent, skirts the danger areas, and all being well, rocks up at Cedric's home town of Grange-over-Sands none the worse for wear. He once escorted the Duke of Edinburgh across the bay in a horse-drawn carriage – upon which His Royal Highness observed:

'This is a remarkable part of the world.'

How right he was. Arnside's full of remarkable people too. Some of them are relative newcomers who've chosen to settle here and run businesses along its delightful promenade. I dallied for lunch at an establishment called Posh Sardine. There was, however, no fish on the menu. Posh Sardine is an anagram of Arnside shop – I should have realised. This café-cum-gift-shop is owned by Jane and Stephen Caldwell who come from Bolton: Jane a chartered surveyor; Stephen a P.E. teacher and middle distance runner who once raced against Sebastian Coe. So why choose Arnside?

'It's quirky,' said Stephen. 'Although we're off the beaten track, we can be on Lake Windermere in 25 minutes. Tourists who clog the roads and fill the hotels in the Lake District have a wonderful base here, if only they realised it. Mind you, we hope they never do.'

A curious sentiment, I thought, for someone who relies on customers. To my astonishment, it was shared by other tradesfolk along Arnside's delightful promenade of shops and cafes. Liz McGonagle, who runs The Little Shop, did her best to explain:

'What we all love about Arnside is the peace and quiet. We don't want anyone to find us and spoil it. It's a thriving little place. More than 2,000 people live here and they're our regular customers. Let's keep it a secret.'

The Caldwells love Arnside's quirkiness.

Former coastguard Tim Cross and his dog Flick.

I realise I'm not helping the cause so apologies, Liz. The village, which was once a popular resort with Lancashire millworkers during Wakes Weeks, has slipped into the background since the industrial decline. Echoing Liz's viewpoint, Lesley at No. 43 is happy to be out of the spotlight. Even without it, she keeps busy, charging up to £185 a night at the most luxurious guest house it's been my pleasure to visit. It has a 5-star gold award. Her customers come from as far away as the USA and Australia to tour the lakes. Lesley relies on repeat business. She doesn't need crowds. In fact crowds can bring problems.

The summer of 2013 was a case in point. A combination of heavy rain in the early months, followed by hot sunshine through July and August made the sands unusually hazardous. It was the worst summer for call-outs Tim Cross could remember:

'People either forgot the sirens or responded in the wrong way by going *onto* the sands instead of leaving them. I saw one woman push her pram along the beach at the foot of the viaduct when the alarm sounded. She must have been off her trolley.'

The incident reminded him of his worst experience as a coastguard. Recounting the story still affects him:

'It was a Sunday morning. We were all at the station for practice, which was very fortunate. We received a call from a fisherman who'd see a couple and their dog in trouble around the headland. He'd tried to rescue them but couldn't. We fired up the 4-wheel drive and the quicksand trailer and raced out. Luckily, the middle-aged woman and her dog had managed to get to the shore. The husband wasn't so lucky. Poor chap was up to his knees in quicksand. He was in shock. With the tide rising, we pumped water into the sand to loosen it and just pulled him out as the water reached his neck. Another ten minutes and we'd have had to abandon him. All our lives were in danger.'

Tim has crossed the sands many times, usually accompanied by Flick. He once received a standing ovation from a small crowd lining the waterfront at Grange-over-Sands. They'd seen him dare to take the short route, dodging the quicksand with consummate expertise.

I met Stephanie Woodburn, an Arnsider for 42 years, who told me that crossing the bay should be a rite of passage for everyone in the village. She announced:

'I've been across three times now. That's the full 6-hour trip. It's wonderful. My children and grand-children have all done it. I think everyone should do it. It's part of what we are.'

I could spend hours absorbing the changing flows of water and subtle shift of colours in the sky. Arnside is a painter's delight. Next time I'll bring my brushes.

Below: Visitors often under-estimate the power of the tides.

TURNED TO STONE

Avebury, Wiltshire

For century after century, in glorious anonymity, the farming folk of Avebury ploughed the fields and scattered good seed on the land. Then along came a playboy archaeologist to catapult them into the spotlight. His name was Alexander Keiller. His mission was to unearth a monument which had lain buried since early mediaeval times. The repercussions are still being felt. As the National Trust literature puts it: 'Avebury may not be Britain's best known stone circle, but being fourteen times the size of Stonehenge, it is undoubtedly the greatest.'

Go to this unique place today and the world goes with you – Americans, Australians, French, Germans and Japanese. 'Too many visitors,' argue the locals, 'They clog the streets and trample the orchids.' I can sympathise. Even a biting Bank Holiday wind, whipping across Wiltshire's broad acres, failed to keep the numbers down. Parents with upturned collars and hands stuffed in pockets ushered disenchanted offspring between giant stone pillars where sheep sheltered from the gusts; a distant drumbeat drew the ear and eye to a ridge against a slate-grey sky upon which a cluster of neo-pagans in Neolithic costume made music; hooded teenagers clutching cans of Stella laughed and squealed as they rolled down the grassy bank of Avebury's prehistoric earthworks, while the less adventurous sought enlightenment at the Henge shop where the latest edition of Crop Circle News was hot off the press.

One hundred and fifty yards – yet light years – away from all of that, Heather Peak-Garland (aged 80+) sat in her period cottage and contemplated the enormous changes which turned her beloved parish into a World Heritage Site. She's one of the few residents who was born and has spent her life in Avebury. When she was a girl, the only visitors were artists who came to paint pretty cottages with honeysuckle around the door. Instead of blinding yellow, fields were a soft shade of gold. Heather's from farming stock. It was her grandfather, James Peak-Garland who allowed Keiller to excavate his land, free of charge, when the quest for the hidden stones began in 1926. Little could historians have known what was to follow.

The stone circles were constructed somewhere between 5,000 and 2,500 BC for reasons that may never be known. Many believe they have a deeply spiritual quality. An American tourist I spoke to thought Neolithic man must have been bored and in need of a project! Most of the stones had been flattened and covered with earth, possibly on the orders of the church. Others were broken up and used in the building trade. Keiller, a marmalade heir from Dundee with a passion for witchcraft, women and archaeology, bought Avebury Manor and started digging. No-one gave the stones a second thought. Rather casual, you might say, because the village was sitting on the most significant – and lucrative – megalithic site in Europe.

Now it's out in the open and Avebury attracts hundreds of thousands of tourists a year. Heather's ambivalent about them *and* the circles. She doesn't like being swamped with people and cars, but she appreciates how vital the stones and the museums Keiller created are to the village economy. She speaks from personal

Avebury Manor almost became a theme park.

We'll never know the significance of the stones.

experience. Heather ran a thriving bed-and-breakfast business for twenty years at St. Andrew's Cottage, her eighteenth-century home:

'I had some wonderful guests. Texans were my favourites, but fancy coming all that way to look at stones and crop circles! I don't personally have any spiritual connection with the stones – and the fascination with crop circles makes me smile. All you need is a stick, a board and a piece of string. The people who make crop circles deserve credit for creating fantastic patterns, but in reality they're vandals and a nuisance to farmers.'

Along with the rest of the true locals, this outspoken octogenarian lives the right side of the tracks – or more accurately, a small brick ramp in the street and a sign which warns: 'No tourists beyond this point.' The ramp is Avebury's version of the Berlin Wall. Twenty-first century Avebury is a combination of retired professionals and what Heather calls 'blow-ins', i.e. newcomers. They commute to Swindon and London. The TV presenter, Ludovic Kennedy lived next door to Heather. He was influential in a fierce dispute which had villagers warring among themselves in 1988/9 and warranted a television documentary.

It concerned an entrepreneur called Ken King who paid a million pounds to buy the dilapidated Avebury Manor and turn it into an 'Elizabethan Experience', complete with musketeers and falconry displays. Kennedy protested on screen; 'He's turning the village into a theme park!' King's response: 'We're recreating the history of this house.' His stoical stance was doomed. Irate 'blow-ins' and obdurate planners helped to land the poor chap in the bankruptcy court. Eventually, the National Trust bought Avebury Manor from the Official Receiver and completed an ambitious makeover in 2011.

'Strange thing,' said Heather, 'on a sunny day, the Manor beckons you in, but on a grey day, it makes you want to run. It's one of the spookiest places I know.'

Then she took her bag and left for the two o'clock bus to Marlborough. She's never learned to drive. There didn't seem much point. Heather more or less grew up on horseback. Public transport means a three-hour round trip for five minutes at the dentist's, but to her it's pleasure:

'I love riding on the top deck of a bus. You get a wonderful view of the Downs. After all these years, I still think I'm surrounded by the most wonderful scenery in England.'

She has a point.

SECRET SUMMERS OF THE ELEPHANT MAN

Badby, Northamptonshire

You'll be surprised to hear me call Northamptonshire a hidden delight. Although it's officially labelled 'The Rose of Shires', the majority of motorists regard it as a county that takes ages to drive through on the M1. They don't see the best bits.

I have news for them. It's as pretty as the Cotswolds! The area between the M1 and the M40 is dotted with thatched cottages of golden ironstone and peppered with timeless villages.

My travels brought me to Badby, halfway been Banbury and Daventry. It's a part of Northamptonshire I hadn't visited since recording a story for the Radio 4 programme *You and Yours* in the 1970s about villages which still relied on wells for their water supplies.

This time, the purpose of my visit was rather different. I'd heard reports that an unusual historical figure had strong connections here. In glorious June sunshine, the facade of Fawsley Hall glowed through the beech trees like a brilliant splash of honey. The landlord of a nearby pub had tipped me off that this part-Victorian, part-Tudor mansion was where the infamous Elephant Man worked as a stablehand. I thought he was joking.

'No,' he responded. 'It's perfectly true. They collected him at Long Buckby railway station and drove him to Fawsley.'

Most people in the Badby/Byfield/Chipping Warden area are unaware of their place in history because visits by this celebrated 'freak' were a closely-guarded secret. For three successive summers towards the end of the 1800s, Redhill Wood

Left: Badby played secret host to a unique and tragic visitor.

which connects the three villages, was home to the Elephant Man, otherwise known as John Merrick. John had been granted his wish to escape the London hospital where he was under permanent supervision and enjoy some time in the countryside. His excursions were made possible by a well-known actress of the day called Madge Kendall. She knew the Knightleys of Fawsley Hall and persuaded them to help a tragic 25 year old hideously deformed by a disease we now know as neurofibromatosis.

Although Madge considered him tragic, John was an intelligent, artistic and well-read young man whose determination and self-esteem remained intact despite years of appalling treatment. I tried to find out why the actress became involved. It's a mystery. However, aristocratic Victorians had a habit of 'collecting' curiosities of all types – including humans. It would have been considered good PR for an actress to adopt such a physically handicapped and downtrodden soul as John Merrick. On the other hand, cynics might argue that Madge and Lady Knightley were only a step removed from voyeurs who paid to ogle John Merrick when he was a circus sideshow. In Lady Knightley's favour, she was a recognised philanthropist. Until the Elephant Man turned up on the estate, she'd never actually met him. He soon became a friend.

John would leave Euston in a blacked-out carriage. When it reached Long Buckby, it was shunted into sidings away from the public gaze. Once the regular passengers had dispersed, he was ushered into a horse-drawn carriage with heavy curtains and taken the short trip to Badby. Staff at Fawsley were warned of what was to come but it proved too much for his first carer. The poor woman was horrified on seeing the Elephant Man. She screamed, threw her apron over her head and ran off. The calmest person around was John Merrick. He was accustomed to such reactions.

During those three summers, he was given the use of a gamekeeper's cottage and more or less left to his own devices. Villagers would occasionally catch a glimpse of him. Some even stopped to pass the time of day. I spoke to Fred Hutt whose father became a 'friend' of the Elephant Man. This is what he remembers:

'Dad told me how intrigued local people were by their summertime guest. They were surprised at his cultured voice and general knowledge. He had trouble pronouncing words because of his deformity, but he had a gentlemanly way with him. In order not to frighten people, he wore a broad-brimmed hat with a veil, rather like a beekeeper.'

Whatever Madge Kendall and Lady Knightley's motives, the visits to Badby were a triumph. Elephant Man loved his rural retreat. His London surgeon, Sir Frederick Treves wrote at the time:

John Meyrick, the Elephant Man

Help for the Elephant Man came from an unlikely source, Fawsley Hall.

'He'd never wandered among fields before, nor followed the windings of a wood. He'd never gathered flowers in a meadow. It was the supreme holiday of his life.'

Elephant Man wrote to Dr. Treves about foxes and badgers he'd seen; daisies he'd picked in Badby woods ; skylarks he'd heard and trout he'd watched darting through the river Cherwell. Of course these simple pleasures were denied to most of townsfolk in those days, but doubly appreciated by someone who spent his life either secreted in a basement or on public show when the circus was in town.

In spite of his physical degeneration, John Merrick remained good humoured until he died in his sleep in 1880, aged 27. Although he was unable to smile or show any facial expression, he frequently told his doctor:

'I'm happy every hour of the day.'

FROM PICNICS TO PARK HOMES

Box Hill, Surrey

Jane Austen tells us that her fictional heroine, Emma 'had never been to Box Hill' and 'wished to see what everybody found so well worth seeing.' She'd be astonished now. The panorama from this striking outcrop of chalk downland is rivalled by the spectacle of day-glow lycra and twitching thighs as hundreds of cyclists urge their carbon fibre machines up the famous Zig Zag. Box Hill, at 735 feet above sea level, attracts more pedal pushers than picnickers these days.

Its reputation was bolstered when the London Olympics Committee selected Box Hill for the final of the men's road race. Sir Bradley Wiggins and company climbed the Zig Zag no fewer than nine times while fifteen thousand spectators lined the hillside. It was the obvious location. Men have tested their lungpower on Box Hill since the bicycle was invented. By the 1890s Dorking Cycling Club was attracting thousands to its cycle camps. Endurance was the name of the game.

In Jane Austen's time, Box Hill presented an altogether more sedate picture. The gentry had discovered eating *al fresco*. Picnics were the height of fashion. This is how London Society magazine of 1876 described a typical scene on the steepest slopes in Surrey:

'The maidens busy themselves with the cloth laying and the setting of knives and forks….unpacking, with much relish, cold pies, chickens, lobsters….bottled Bass, sherry, claret….not even omitting a few borage leaves.'

That was more Emma's style. Having a picnic on Box Hill today lacks subtlety. Burgers, chips and ice cream have replaced lobster and borage. Victorian townies once sought higher ground to escape the fetid air of the city. Today's townies queue for the pay-and-display car park and the numerous fast food outlets. The nearest elevated beauty spot to London attracts a million visitors a year.

And yet, out of sight and almost out of mind on the summit, Box Hill *village* gets on with its everyday life. Most people don't even know there is a village. Mandy and Gary Ayling were exceptions. They knew. They'd

Left: Box Hill, beloved of Jane Austen, is where the gentry discovered the joys of eating al fresco.

had their eye on it for years. Gary was a postman in nearby Banstead. Few things escaped his attention. He and his wife dreamed of living in Box Hill Village. Their chance arrived in 2009 when Box Hill Country Store came onto the market. It's just off the main road and therefore protected from the constant stream of bikes and cars. Tourists are a small part of their customer base. Says Gary:

'They get what they need at the pub, the snack bars and the Visitor Centre. Our trade is local. This village is a retirement catchment. Unlike the rest of the hill, it's very quiet. We have a lovely way of life. What other people come to enjoy at weekends is ours all the time. Driving up the Zig Zag on a summer's evening makes you glad to be alive.'

There are a few stately piles in Box Hill Village but seventy five per cent of the 2,300 residents live *in mobile homes*. I've never seen so many. The village feels more like a transit camp than a permanent fixture. It goes back to the 1950s when it boasted a large open-air swimming pool with an adjoining caravan park where families would spend their summer holidays. Then the site was converted into park homes to cater for the post-war London overspill. Make no mistake though, these park homes are a bit tasty. Some of them are valued at £250,000. The reason? Location, location, location.

The Downs, the clean air and the forest of box trees which gave the hill its name are only part of the story. Villagers have an embarrassment of other attractions on their doorstep. This is where John Logie Baird invented television. In the 1930s, the great innovator conducted many of his early experiments at Swiss Cottage, his aptly named home high up on the hill. Then there's the Fort, built to protect London from European invaders but never required. Soldiers were instructed to wear slippers because the Fort was packed with gunpowder. A single spark from a military boot striking the stone floor would have ignited most of Surrey!

The Fort's now home to three species of bats which thrive in the tunnel. The surrounding meadows are illuminated in midsummer by a dozen rare orchids and a plethora of butterflies. If you look closely you'll also find the upside down grave of Major Peter Labilliere. The esteemed Major was convinced that the world was topsy-turvy and would eventually right itself. He therefore insisted on being buried vertically with his head pointing downwards. Box Hill is no ordinary place.

Left: The Men's Olympic Road Race climbs Box Hill, 2012.

SOME CORNER OF AN ENGLISH FIELD
THAT IS FOREVER HELMAND

Brecklands, Norfolk

The smell of goat curry drifts across the square. Villagers scurry to the mosque as the call to prayer crackles through the microphone. It's good to be in Norfolk.

This isn't a joke. It concerns 25,000 acres of England coloured white on the Ordnance Survey map. The map shows no roads, no villages and no markings of any sort. Odd. If there'd been such a map in the 1930s, it would have shown villages like Buckenham Tofts, Langford, Stanford, Tottington and West Tofts. Countryfolk scratched a living from a large, sandy heath called Brecklands. Most of them were tenants of Lord Walsingham at Walsingham Hall. None of them, including the local squire, had any idea what was in store for them.

Above: Since when was war declared on Norfolk? It's littered with decaying armoured vehicles at Brecklands.

It's hard to believe this undulating expanse of gorse and grassland, dotted with sheep and bordered by regimented rows of Scots pine, is now a battlefield. What could have happened? Here's a clue: – Colonel Tony Powell granted me the rare privilege of a tour of the Stanford Training Area, as it's called. It's the only Ministry of Defence site in Britain entirely barred to the public. Twenty five thousand acres of Norfolk have effectively been frozen in time for more than 60 years – except that, as Colonel Powell pointed out, the MoD continually manages and develops the land.

In the middle distance I see a field under polythene. 'Carrots', said the colonel. He explained that a dozen tenant farmers grow their crops and tend their livestock here. Even then, they cannot come and go as they wish. Nobody except the troops have unlimited access. Ten marines jogged past us. They looked completely out of place.

The Brecklands underwent a metamorphosis in 1942, halfway through the Second World War. Unsuspecting peasants were told to report to the blacksmith's forge in West Tofts at ten o'clock one momentous morning. They were told they had three weeks to get out. The army needed the land to prepare for the growing menace of Adolf Hitler. At a stroke, Buckenham Tofts, Langford, Stanford, Tottington and West Tofts were wiped off the map. I've heard that the sacrificial villagers were promised a speedy return to their homes once the war was over, but there's no official record of such a promise.

They never did go back. Brecklands became a sinister version of Disneyland. First they built a Nazi village so that troops could familiarise themselves with the German landscape. As conflict moved to different parts of the globe in the ensuing years, the MoD constructed a Bosnian equivalent, followed by an Iraqi village and, most recently – and most adventurously – an Afghan village, pieced together in 2009 at a cost of £14 million.

Colonel Powell drove me there in the army Land Rover. He's immensely proud of the Afghan village, as well he might be. When it's in active service, no fewer than 650 Afghan refugees are recruited to camp here, use the cooking areas, tether their goats and operate a series of make-believe stalls stocking plastic fruit and empty tins with Afghan labels. The single-storey houses around the square are authentic. So are the alleys. They're designed to present soldiers with communication difficulties. The makeshift mosque and a sewage ditch complete the picture.

While I absorbed the ambiance, Colonel Powell took me to see the only church remaining from pre-military days. The colonel has a special interest in St. Mary's at West Tofts. It's one of Britain's best examples of a Pugin church and it comes to life every Christmas when 400 invited guests gather for a carol service. Among them until recently were two cousins evacuated from the old village. Age eventually caught up with Esmie and Marion.

Remarkably, with the help of a £250,000 grant from English Heritage, Colonel Powell was able to oversee the return of St. Mary's magnificent stained glass window. The MoD had replaced it with plain glass in 1942, sending the original to be kept in boxes at Ely Stained Glass Museum. It was reconstituted like a giant jigsaw and reinstated for the 60th anniversary of military rule.

English Heritage agreed to stump up the money on condition that the MoD hold twelve open days a year for the public to familiarise themselves with this extraordinary story and, where relevant, pay their respects to lost relatives. Descendants of displaced families were able to revisit the abandoned cottages. A few are left but most have been reduced by the elements to grassy humps. Once rainwater got through holes in the roof, degeneration was swift.

The Army's commandeering of the heath and the villages has always been a sensitive issue. Depending on your point of view, it was either brutal or vital. There wasn't time to mount much of a resistance. A spirited lass called Lucilla Reeve tried hard but she was a lone voice. Lucilla wrote the book, *Farming on a Battlefield* in which she recounted the full story. The author became increasingly isolated. Paranoia took over. Lucilla barricaded herself in a henhouse and eventually took her own life. That act (illegal at the time) meant that she couldn't be buried in consecrated ground. To compensate, the MoD has since extended the cemetery fence to include Lucilla's grave.

Colonel Powell drove me past the steps to a manor house which has long since vanished, and three former council houses with new tin roofs. Then he braked. Pointing to the horizon, the colonel puffed out his chest and said:

'Doesn't that look fabulous? English countryside the way it used to be before telegraph poles and mobile phone masts.'

I had to agree.

The village is often deserted.

It comes to life when 650 Afghan refugees are bussed in.

Remnants of old Tottington village survive.

PHALLIC ATTRACTION

Cerne Abbas, Dorset

Is there more to Cerne Abbas than an excited giant carved in the chalk? Has this fertility symbol made any difference to the birth rate? I set off for the far corners of Dorset to find out.

Little Cerne Abbas was propelled onto the world stage in the seventeenth century when an unknown artist (assisted no doubt by a few pals) left a suggestive piece of graffiti on the hillside. It was a 180 feet tall figure of a naked man wielding a club and displaying his enlarged manhood. Creating the image was a painstaking business. They dug out the soil and replaced it with crushed chalk.

The Cerne Abbas Giant has been the village meal ticket ever since. Scholars still argue about its spiritual significance while bashful ladies avert their gaze. A 1920s vicar thought it obscene and begged the Home Secretary to plough it up. Luckily for the local economy, the politician turned a deaf ear. Visitors pour in to see it. Three splendid alehouses and a village shop grow slightly plumper if not exactly fat on the proceeds.

Dorset lives in a world of its own. Turn off the arterial A303 to Exeter and you're immediately into narrow country roads threaded between curvaceous chalk downs. You're competing with tractors. Cattle are being herded from field to field. There are eggs for sale at every other farm gate. Thomas Hardy got it just right. *Far From the Madding Crowd* couldn't be more apropos. Cerne Abbas actually appears in Thomas Hardy's Wessex, but under the assumed name of Abbots Cernel. It also topped the charts as Britain's Most Desirable Village in a 2008 survey by the estate agents, Savills.

I hesitate to say it but my first experience was disappointing. I headed straight for the viewing platform at the foot of the famous hill but could barely make out the

Left: Tourists flock to this sleepy village for reasons they'd perhaps rather keep to themselves.

shape of the giant. Several tourists seemed equally bemused. Maybe it was the light or more likely the grass needed cutting. I must have a word with the National Trust who own the site.

Nevertheless, the sun lit up one side of Long Street, Cerne Abbas' main thoroughfare and the village basked quietly in its superlatives. Quietly? There was a deathly silence. Then I discovered why. They were all in the pubs. There are three: *The Giant, The Royal Oak,* and the architecturally enticing *New Inn*, built of brick, flint *and* stone. If three pubs for one village seems greedy, consider that in its well-lubricated heyday, Cerne Abbas boasted no fewer than *fourteen* taverns. Ale brewed in the village from Dorset's pristine chalk streams was eagerly quaffed as far away as London in the 1800s. Beer rivalled The Rude Giant as Cerne's greatest claim to fame.

The nearest brewery today is over the hill in the Piddle Valley but I'm pleased to say that the *New Inn*, which accounted for most of the people who'd vanished off the streets, was doing its best to keep the regional flag flying. On tap was a local brew from Bridport, only fifteen miles away. The pub was extraordinarily busy for Wednesday lunchtime. The blackboard menu included relative novelties like beetroot soufflé and braised shoulder of rabbit. The tenant, Jeremy Lee was bonhomie personified. He told me:

'Cerne Abbas was a sleepy hollow when I came here. The Inn was at death's door. A spit-and-sawdust boozer. Now we're unashamedly foodie with a dozen luxury bedrooms, 75,000 links on our website and a good income from weekend breaks.'

How much of that was down to the giant on the hill?

'A lot. But visitors go for the whole Dorset package. River walks, Jurassic coast, fabulous countryside.'

On hearing that I was researching this book, one of the diners, an ex-pat over from Western Australia tapped me on the shoulder. Did I know that Dorset was the only county without a motorway?

I thanked her for her enthusiasm but pointed out that at least two more counties – Cornwall and Lincolnshire – were similarly blessed. Nice try though. My informant had been away from the area for 25 years and was intrigued to know why eggs were being given away at the farm gate. I asked her what she meant.

'Well,' she replied, 'the sign says Free – Range Eggs, whatever they are.'

Ha! ha! A lot has changed in 25 years. But on the subject of 'foreigners', I noticed an array of international newspapers at the village store. They'd have done justice to a kiosk in central London. Apart from Le Figaro, shoppers could buy Die Welt, Corriere della Sera, USA Today – and a couple of Arab dailies. In demure little Cerne Abbas? What was that all about? The shopkeeper said the journals were mainly for tourists but that a few regulars were second-home owners who commuted two or three times a week to London. They lapped them

A former local vicar begged the Home Secretary to dig it up, but the chalk man drives the prosperity of the high street.

up. Sherborne station is a short drive away and deposits you at Waterloo in two hours. The fingers of modernity reach closer than Hardy would ever have dreamed.

First question answered then. There *is* more to Cerne Abbas than a phallic symbol. And that's without talking you through lovely old buildings like Abbot's Porch, the Tithe Barn and the Pitchmarket where farmers pitched their corn sacks for inspection on market day.

That brings us to the fertility question. I consulted the font of all wisdom, George Mortimer, chairman of the Historical Society. He said the birth rate hadn't risen noticeably in the last 200 years. In fact the reverse was true. When Cerne Abbas was bypassed by the railway, the population plummeted. A busy brewery and farming town became a quiet village. George added:

'More than half the village is over 65 so I can't see the numbers going up. Mind you, we do have a thriving primary school.'

Interesting. So don't run away with the idea that Cerne Abbas is stuck in the past. On the contrary, it's a forward-thinking place. On the wall of the *New Inn* is a certificate from the *Good Pub Guide* announcing that Jeremy Lee's establishment won Dorset's 'Dining Pub of the Year 2014' competition. Congratulations Jeremy, but they've got the date wrong. We're still in 2013. He laughed:

'They always do it that way. We like to stay ahead of the game around here.'

Fair enough.

BY INVITATION ONLY

Churchend, Foulness, Essex

There was a shiver of anticipation as we sailed up the estuaries of the Crouch and Roach and caught our first sight of the mystery island. Essex has several islands but this one's different. On our arrival, a family of seals plopped into the water as if to say: 'It's all yours, folks.'

Our ship's captain, Brian Dawson dropped anchor and signalled us to man the rowboat. It felt mischievous and secretive – like a sequel to the D-Day landings. A few strokes of the oar took us to the quay. We clambered up the seaweed and gazed across a windy, treeless landscape dotted with poles and radar towers. A place of beauty and decay. Brian stayed on the quay to keep an eye on the boats. I told him half jokingly that if we weren't back in an hour, we'd been arrested.

An ancient by-law states that sailors can access Foulness island at this particular point when red flags aren't flying. It's one of those anomalies. Access by road is prohibited but boat people can wander around at leisure as long as they keep to the footpaths. It's been that way since the War Office bought Foulness in 1915. Seven thousand acres of real estate are fenced off from the rest of the country as though it were a leper colony. Yet 135 civilians live, work and bring up their children here.

They're concentrated in two hamlets, Churchend and Courtsend, which, uniquely, were allowed to remain intact when the military moved in. There's no other MoD site in the UK where civilians and squaddies operate cheek by jowl. Security is so tight that, a few years ago, a *newly elected MP* couldn't even get past the gatehouse. He waited three months for permission to meet his constituents!

Back on the northeast shore, we saw a footpath sign pointing towards Churchend and walked for twenty minutes through fields of parched rapeseed waiting to be harvested. Buzzards swirled and called high above us. There are endless amounts of food for them in a semi-wilderness. Despite the bangs and the flying shells, birdlife prospers in this precarious environment. The name Foulness is a corruption of the Anglo-Saxon Fuglanaes, meaning Wild Bird Promontory.

Above: This is the most exclusive village in Britain. It's out of bounds to you and me.

The sun was getting warmer. The sense of isolation increased as we headed inland. A church spire appeared on the horizon and beyond it, two white buildings which turned out to be the *George and Dragon* pub and the post office. We made a beeline for the pub, surprised that we'd got this far unchallenged. Liquid refreshment wasn't the immediate concern. I was more interested to know how a hostelry could survive in no-man's-land. The resident population was too small to keep it going and there was no passing trade. Customers from the mainland could only access the *George and Dragon* by private arrangement with the landlord and Qinetiq, the agency managing Foulness on behalf of the MoD. As I expected, pub takings were at rock bottom. The landlord was losing hope. It was only a matter of time.

If you like living dangerously, you can come this way.

Empty shells litter the shore.

The church: closed for business.

That was my first visit to Foulness in 2005. By 2013, the residents of Churchend, endeavouring as ever to keep in touch with the rest of society, took matters into their own hands. With the help of a lottery grant, they modernised the Heritage Centre (formerly the primary school) and persuaded Qinetiq that public open days on the first Sunday of each month between April and October would be a good thing. It was a major shift change and a sizeable boost to the islanders' morale. So, having once negotiated the seaward passage, I opted for the more formal approach this time.

I queued at the gate for my pass on the first Sunday in August and was joined by members of the Southend Classic Car Club, most of whom had never set foot on the island. A cavalcade of Vauxhall Crestas, Triumph Heralds and Ford Anglias crossing over the bridge and down the forbidden highway would have been unthinkable ten years ago. We passed gun batteries named after farms – Shelford, Priestwood and Rugwood. They were built next to designated conservation areas where oyster-catchers pecked at the mudflats. Acres of wheat stood tall and swayed in the breeze. The air was salty. Gulls and curlews provided the sound effects.

'We enjoy this as much as the visitors,' said John Burroughs, a Churchend stalwart who recognised me from my previous visit. He was doing his stint in the Heritage Centre Museum. John and his two brothers farm 8,000 acres in the middle of the island. The family's been at it since 1946. He remembers when the islanders were self-sufficient. They trapped rabbits, caught fish and shot wildfowl. All their vegetables were home grown. These days they rely on the Co-op at Great Wakering across the water. John was pleased with the open-day turnout:

'Open days bring life to the island. It's also a chance for ex-islanders to reconnect. As you can see, we're passionate about this place. There's nowhere like it. We're sworn to secrecy about some of its history but I can tell you they researched the atom bomb here during the Cold War. They still test shells by firing them into the sea. We're evacuated twelve times a year, usually for a day at a time. We've grown up with it. It's part of the Foulness experience.'

Left: Farmers and soldiers live side by side.

John's 15-year-old son, Jack nodded in agreement. I expected him to complain about lack of activity for young people in such a deserted place. Instead, he enthused about the farm and said he'd be ready to take over from his dad when the time came. As we talked, the aptly named Peter Carr pulled up in his highly-prized Morgan and parked it next to a Bullnose Morris. He'd be conducting the tractor tour. I bought a ticket just in time. It was a sell-out. Peter farms here too. The soil is famously fertile. They first realised that in the sixteenth century and land grabbers moved in. By the late 1700s, nearly 800 people lived on Foulness.

Today, all the cottages and farmhouses are rented from the MoD. That goes for the *George and Dragon* too. The pub closed down not long after my previous visit. The school ran out of steam several years earlier. The church is also out of action. Services are held in people's homes. Luckily, the post office/shop defies this downward trend.

Peter fired up his tractor and off we went. Foulness in its August plumage of gold, cream and beige, looked serene. The passengers were silent, absorbing the mood. We tried to imagine red flag days when the island's at its most explosive. They account for Mondays to Thursdays with half days on Friday. A replica of the doorway to number 10 Downing Street was once exploded to see how it would stand up to a terrorist attack. Shells destined for British engagement overseas are tested every week. Bomb disposal officers train here. Ordnance huts and batteries are scattered among the wild flowers.

The driver stopped by a gap in the sea wall and showed us where London's third airport was once due to be built on Maplin Sands. The danger of unexploded shells might have deterred Ted Heath's government. At any rate, the plans were shelved. Two wind farms glow in the distance. One is close to Clacton on Sea; the other close to Margate. A rocky causeway stretches out in front of us. It disappears into the sea after a few hundred yards, reappears further out as a sandbank then vanishes again. This was the notorious Broomway, Foulness's only connection with the mainland before they built a road in 1957. The causeway is lined with empty shells, once fired into the sea, recovered then left to rust on the mud.

Since there was no security presence at this point, it occurred to me that public access might still be possible along the Broomway. My enquiries confirmed that anyone prepared to walk for seven miles across Maplin Sands could indeed come and go by this route – but only at weekends, before 6.30 am or after 5.30 pm when the MoD isn't firing. Otherwise, the barrier's down at the Great Wakering end of the Broomway.

After enthralling his customers with a mixture of history and folklore, Peter drove us through the second village of Courtsend. The village consisted of a dozen houses, mostly clad in weatherboarding. There was no sign of life. Further on, we passed a run-down farmhouse half-buried in crops.

One of the passengers uttered the thoughts of many:

'That's beautiful. I could live there.'

But she'd have a lot of work to do first. Or rather, the MoD would, if it wanted to restore the listed building. As its name implies, Brick House with its red slate roof and period outbuildings was the island's first brick house in 1700. It's been empty for 40 years. Part of the roof has perished. That'll soon affect the interior. According to our guide, Brick House is 'wonderful' inside. Timbered walls and ceilings; inglenook fireplace; a bread oven and a brew house. It's crying out for TLC but the MoD doesn't listen. Nor has it shown any enthusiasm for restoring the *George and Dragon*, despite several would-be landlords making their interest known. Ironically, the pub would have been busy that particular Sunday. When we got back to the Heritage Centre, there must have been 200 visitors craving lunch and a pint or three.

I had a chat with Peter, whom I'd also met before. He told me the islanders were concerned about the number of empty houses:

'Initially we thought it was the MoD's way of saying they don't want us around any more. If they allowed the villages to run down, they could have the island to themselves. To be honest, it's a miracle we're here at all. On any other MoD site we'd have been sent packing. Thankfully two vacant cottages have just been let, so the population's going up. Perhaps our fears are unfounded.'

He said the inconvenience of living on an explosive island was balanced by the safety and security that comes with being permanently under guard. Crime doesn't exist. Peter's worst moment came last summer; -

'They were casseroling a bomb for a week. That means heating it up and letting it cool down to see how it would react in a fire. It happened close to my land so we had to leave. Unfortunately the pea aphid arrived at the same time and I couldn't spray my crop. By the time we were given the all-clear to return, the peas were in a sorry state. I lost a third of them.'

He smiled when I brought up the subject of compensation:

'Haha! I'm afraid there's nothing like that. We grin and bear it. It's a small price to pay for the pleasure of being here.'

Visitors had to be off the island by 4.00pm. Churchend would be unplugged until the next open day. After two more Sundays it would be out of contact for six months. Unless of course someone arrived by boat.

LIFE ON THE TILT

Clovelly, Devon

With the possible exception of Machu Picchu, Clovelly is the most gravity-defying place you'll come across. The village was built on the hypotenuse of a north Devon cliff – the equivalent of a black run at St. Moritz. Eighty white-walled cottages dangle oceanwards like pearls on a woman's sternum.

Needless to say, there are no vehicles. Inhabitants drag their goods up and down the cobbles on wooden sledges – groceries, pots and pans, furniture, ageing relatives etc. There's a sledge parked against every front door. The *New Inn Hotel* has an open-fronted bar carved out of the rock; the Post Office is still there but had its status reduced in 2011. Fisherman's Cottage (now a museum) is well worth the trip. So is the house where Charles Kingsley wrote *The Water Babies*. Kingsley adored Clovelly. Two-thirds of the way down the hill, the 'road' becomes more like the chute of a helter-skelter. It – and you – plunge between the houses until you reach the harbour a hundred feet below.

The tide was out as we headed towards the quay to enjoy Clovelly's annual Lobster and Crab Feast. Early visitors climbed up and down the big stone steps of the harbour wall, balancing seafood lunches and jugs of local cider. Dogs and children splashed in the mud around upturned fishing boats tethered by chains. The sun shone warmly. There was a strong smell of seaweed. From the bottom looking up, Clovelly was even more improbable. Someone once described it as 'a long, irregular white scar in a dark green cheek.'

A fiddler began to play. A group of folk singers joined in. Live and dead lobsters were selling for £10 on the main stall. Nearby a crab was being dressed. And all the time, the serpent of tourists down the zig-zag path grew longer and longer. Fortunately, stallholders, musicians and chefs were spared this precarious descent. They couldn't bring their clobber down on a sledge. For them, a sinuous road around the back of the village and a car

park behind *The Red Lion* hotel. It's usually reserved for guests, fisherman and, if they're lucky, long-established families who live in the harbour cottages. There's also a fare-paying Land Rover service for those who don't relish the climb back up the cobbles.

Naturally, the gradient and the tightly-packed cottages aren't everyone's cup of tea. People are all on top of each other. Privacy is at a premium; seclusion non-existent. One resident said:

'Clovelly's the nearest thing to an island without being one.'

He should know. He lived on Lundy for several years before being lured ashore by Clovelly's eccentricity. The island analogy refers to the village's isolation. Residents can't pop to the supermarket or the bank at the drop of a hat. Everything must be planned in advance. The car is probably several hundred yards away at the top of the hill. Bad weather can imprison them. An extreme flood in 2011 turned the 'road' into a waterfall. Houses were flooded and cobbles washed away. It presented the Lord of the Manor, John Rous, with the most difficult task he'd faced since taking over the estate in 1987. It also underlined the village's susceptibility.

In short, it's a thoroughly inconvenient anchorage. Its beauty is the consolation. Gardens are small but brimming with bright shrubs. The surrounding woodlands make a marvellous backdrop. Ellie Jarvis, a textile artist, moved from London six years ago. She and her husband are bringing up two young children in a village where you have to carry your babies on your back. Buggies don't work. When teaching toddlers to take their first step, you have to accept that gravity might overwhelm them. However, rumours that Clovellians have one leg shorter than the other don't stand up! Nor do they sometimes.

Ellie's rose-tinted glasses show no sign of losing their hue. If anything, they're getting rosier. She enthused:

'We're privileged to call this home. When I draw the curtains and look out to the sea, I have to pinch myself. Whether there's brilliant sunshine, moonlight, mist or an Atlantic storm – it doesn't matter. They're all magical. My four-year-old son loves the folklore. He's convinced he's a pirate!'

Like everyone else in Clovelly, (landlord excluded) Ellie's a tenant. This is a privately-owned village. It's been in the same family since 1738. John Rous' weekly 'to do' list would discourage weaker mortals, but he carries his responsibilities with a smile. He still gets a thrill when surveying the family estate from Clovelly Court, a lofty vantage point where he lives. John always has and always will resist the temptation to sell his properties. It's not even a temptation.

Left: Clovelly high street can only be tackled on foot.

Above: This north Devon gem has been in the same family for nearly 300 years.

'We don't want weekenders. They'd kill the place. I want to hand Clovelly on to my daughters as a living, working community. Families with children are the present and the future. The village has to wash its face as a business, and not from the sale of its properties. It's a fun challenge.'

There are several arms to the business – two hotels, a visitor centre, the shops and the harbour, as well as Clovelly Court Gardens. The fisheries are privately owned. Mackerel and herring have traditionally been the main catch but there are currently four lobster fishermen making a decent living. Although they can't fish within a certain radius of Lundy because it's a wildlife conservation area, the Bristol Channel still provides a decent harvest.

Therein a disappointment. As far as I could tell, the lobsters at the Lobster and Crab Feast were bred at an inshore fishery at Padstow, rather than caught in the pots stacked up against the harbour wall in Clovelly. Perhaps the local catch was already spoken for. It's one of life's ironies that Clovellians seldom get a chance to buy their own fish because there's no fish market. Lobster, mackerel, herring and bass go either to *The Red Lion* or to outside suppliers.

For all that, the food was as delicious as we expected – and the cider better than we imagined. We rounded off the day with a visit to the Silk Shop at the top of the village. You can see live silk worms feeding off the leaves of a mulberry tree. It never ceases to astonish me that one of the world's finest textiles is produced by one of its most insignificant creatures. The shop is run by Ellie Jarvis' parents, both of whom trained at Liberty's. By chance they came across fabric from the 1930s featuring drawings by Rex Whistler. The flamboyant artist had been a guest of a previous estate owner, Christine Hamlin, who helped to rebuild Clovelly when it was in a sorry state. Rex's drawings of the village were incorporated into a special fabric in 1932 but the material disappeared for decades until Ellie's parents discovered it in their cottage and revived the tradition. Said Ellie:

'What's so magical is that all these years later, the scenes are more or less identical. Clovelly hasn't changed a jot. Mind you, I still haven't seen a mermaid.'

All in good time, Ellie.

Above: The village lobster and crab festival is the highlight of the year.

Right: Sadly, Clovellians don't get to buy their own seafood.

WELL AND TRULY KIPPERED

Craster, Northumberland

Craster is an easy place to find. You follow your nostrils along the coast from Amble and there, above a picturesque harbour, you'll see and smell the clouds issuing from Robson's famous smokehouse. You've arrived in kipperland. It may not be *L'Air du Temps* but the pong is equally alluring. It conjures images of fishing boats on slate grey seas and American Indians clustered around campfires – at least, it does when you are familiar with the story.

Several places in Britain are synonymous with food. Stilton with cheese (*see* page 159); Pontefract with liquorice cakes; Bakewell with tarts; Melton Mowbray with pork pies, and so on. But Craster has a romance all of its own. To Northumberland folk it's a fishing village. To everyone else it's a tasty breakfast served with tea and hot buttered toast. In the days when trains had chefs and kitchens, I frequently ordered a 'Craster' on the 7.30 from Kings Cross to Newcastle. There are few finer things than kippers for breakfast while the world floats past your window. Preparing them at home is best done in a field – unless your partner's a fan.

For more than 130 years, the reputation of Craster kippers drifted across Britain like the smoke from its curing sheds. You can order them in John o' Groats; you can pick the bones out in Wolverhampton; you can savour the fillets on the Isle of Wight. Word has it that royalty once bought them where royalty shops – in Fortnum and Masons. It's a facility no longer available. F&M insisted on kippers being delivered the same day – apparently missing the point that herrings are smoked in order to make them last.

Before 9/11 you could order them in the breakfast bars of Berlin, Hamburg, Moscow and Leningrad. However, the explosion of the twin towers led to a tightening-up of import and export controls which meant long delays at customs, which in turn persuaded the Robson family to concentrate on the UK market.

Crasters are generally regarded as the best kippers in the world, though some will argue the case for the Manx version. And we mustn't forget Craster's neighbours in Seahouses. *They* also produce a mean kipper – smaller and allegedly sweeter than down the coast. But I'm sorry, a Craster is a Craster. End of story. According to Clarissa Dickson-Wright, comparing it to other kippers is as pointless as comparing Chateaubriand to a McDonalds quarter pounder!

A trip to the smokehouse is always appealing – at least to me. There's something primeval about rack after rack of fish suspended from tenterhooks (the origin of the expression) and turning gold over the slow burn of oak sawdust. And to think it all began in the American west when native Indians, presented with a glut of meat and fish at certain times of the year, invented ways of making it last beyond its season.

The smokehouse is a dream subject for painters and photographers, talking of which, I came across Mick Oxley, a former schoolteacher who runs the village art gallery. You'd think the scope for selling paintings in a small fishing village would be somewhat restricted. Mick does okay though. He reinvented himself as an artist after being struck by M.E. in the late 1980s. Being wheelchair-bound doesn't stop him capturing Northumberland's 'savagely beautiful' seascapes on canvas. Nor does it stop him running a gallery filled with jewellery, metalwork and woodwork as well as paintings. He told me:

'It's been tough lately. When you're worried about your job, you're not going to buy paintings. We're still in business though. '

Naturally, the smokehouse has appeared in some of his work. It's hard to avoid. Says Mick:

'Robsons are an integral part of this village. At one time, half the population worked there. They were called 'herring girls'. Now there are only fifteen on the payroll. Although we sometimes take it for granted, we're proud of our kipper tradition. It's still the main tourist attraction.'

And therefore an important source of customers for Mick's gallery. As indeed it is to Harbour Lights, Peter Howard's small bed and breakfast establishment, not to mention the *Jolly Fisherman*, Craster's village tavern, renowned in local circles for offering gourmet alternatives to the ubiquitous herring!

Craster is the gateway to Dunstanburgh Castle.

Clearly, tourists don't have to spend *all* their time staring at suspended fish. The coastal walk to Dunstanburgh Castle, which can't be reached any other way, is well worth the effort, as indeed is a trip to nearby Alnwick Castle, immortalised in Harry Potter.

But back to the kippers, a seemingly endless font of fascination. Alan Robson, the Godfather of this ancient business certainly thinks so. Every day without fail, the 87-year-old reports for duty at the smokehouse, protesting that he'd be at home watching daytime television if it wasn't for the kippers. Much of the machinery's familiar to him. Some outdates him. But an awful lot has changed since Alan's grandfather James took the plunge in 1906 and bought the building from the Craster family after years of renting it.

Supplies of the raw material dried up in the 1970s, necessitating a change of strategy. North Sea herrings had been plundered to such an extent that the government imposed a ban. It lasted for seven years during which time many smokeries in the North Shields area went out of business. Robson's would have gone the same way if they hadn't switched their attention to fisheries on the west coast of Scotland. It guaranteed them a year-round supply which was essential for maintaining their contract with Waitrose. The supermarket now absorbs 45 per cent of Robson's output.

Kippers have been in the Robson family since 1906.

Alan's son, Neil, is in charge these days. For a time, the world was his oyster, so to speak. His horizons stretched far beyond Northumberland. Then things changed. He said:

'I wasn't channelled into the family business, but after gaining a business studies degree, I decided this is where I wanted to be. I spent my childhood in Craster. There aren't many more beautiful parts of England. But when we moved the family home a few miles away to Howick, it left only five local residents in the village. Most of the houses are holiday lets. The school closed, the shop closed and the bus service was taken away. It seemed as though Craster had disappeared.'

In typically understated fashion – but to the dismay of the workforce – Robson's barely celebrated their centenary in 2006. Perhaps they didn't want to tempt fate. In an era of multinational takeovers, family businesses of that vintage not only deserve enormous respect – they've become collectors' items! In this case, the secret is simple: choose the plumpest fish, smoke them over whitewood shavings and oak sawdust for 16 hours, and you too could start a dynasty. The line looks set to continue. One or both of Neil's daughters should soon be at the helm.

One thing's absolutely clear – it's no use relying on the family for trade. Although Alan Robson eats kippers once a fortnight, the rest of the clan and workforce can't be relied on. Neil only eats one when the mood takes him and Susan Nisbet, receptionist and secretary at the smokehouse for the past 29 years, is of a similar persuasion. She confessed under oath:

'When you see them every day, they lose their appeal. I cook a kipper on the barbecue once a year and swill it down with a glass of wine. That'll do me.'

Personally speaking, I still love them, though I've yet to try the recipe on the company website. Kipper toasties consist of fillets mixed with Cheddar cheese, Worcester sauce and double cream, then toasted on granary bread. I'm off to the kitchen.

SIGNING OFF

Downham, Lancashire

There's little sign of Downham till you get there. And when you do, there's no sign that you've arrived. This dreamy location in the Ribble Valley is the only place I know without a village sign. Effectively it's incognito. Slightly mysterious, but that's only a fraction of the story. Neither are there any television aerials, obtrusive satellite dishes, overhead wires or even road markings. Downham hasn't changed since the 1950s. The cars are the only giveaway.

You could be excused for thinking that it had lost touch with reality, or that the decks had been cleared for filming a period drama ('Downham' Abbey perhaps?) But you'd be wrong. Although film and television producers have taken advantage of its unspoilt scenery in the past, the village looks like this because succeeding Lord Clitheroes have decreed it.

The present incumbent, Ralph Assheton has recently taken over responsibility for the estate from his ageing father. As well as managing Downham, Ralph runs a wood-chip business on the estate and stays a little more in touch with village life than dad. He had this to say about the aversion to street furniture: –

'It's not so much a philosophy, more a wish to conserve nice things and avoid the ugly bits. As soon as you put up a sign for something, you need another sign to explain it. We agreed to a bus timetable next to the telephone box, but there's no sign for the bus stop. We don't need it.'

Although the 'unnamed' village is only three miles from the market town of Clitheroe, we're in Lancashire's finest countryside. It's too dramatic to be called pretty and Downham, for all its limestone beauty, is too 'natural' to decorate a chocolate box. That's not a criticism. Plain and simple makes a welcome change from over-manicured verges and roses around *every* door. There's a mediaeval order to Downham. The church and manor sit on the crest of a ridge. Thirty two estate cottages are neatly arranged in two groups, one below Downham Hall and the other around the main street and village stream.

Shimmering, or sometimes glowering in the background, is Pendle Hill, an isolated mountain detached from the Pennines and standing 1,827 feet above sea level. It's a moody place, beloved of hikers but synony-

mous with witches. In 1610, Downham was indirectly involved in Britain's most notorious witchcraft trial. The case of the Pendle Witches resulted in ten women being hanged for a series of murders in what was then classified as bandit country. North-east Lancashire resembled the tribal areas of Waziristan – wild and lawless. You didn't go there if longevity was your aim. Witches and warlocks lurked around every rock. The air was thick with flying broomsticks.

One of the witches, a certain Alice Nutter, was said to be hiding in Downham Old Hall when she was wanted for trial at Lancaster. It's been suggested that Alice was guilty of 'nothing more sinister than being a vegetarian spinster who owned a black cat.' Evidence presented at the trial had little to do with fact and a lot to do with hearsay and superstition. The witches would have walked free today.

The Assheton family took ownership of Downham estate in 1558, almost fifty years before the celebrated trial. It's been in their hands ever since. Currently there are 32 rented homes, a flourishing pub/restaurant called the *Assheton Arms* and a post office-cum tearoom. Several villagers have expressed an interest in reviving its fortunes should Lord Clitheroe deem it necessary. In the meantime, he's getting used to the idea of 'playing God', or 'balancing the population' as it's more commonly known. He seems to be getting it right. Out of a population of 100, there's a three way split between over-65s, thirtysomethings and under-18s.

For a time, Downham was notable for its barter scheme. A case of 'you cut my hair and I'll wash your car'. It's called Time Bank and it originally operated on a credit/debit system like any other bank. I've seen similar schemes come and go. At Stiperstones in Shropshire, they even issued cheque books in their own currency. It didn't last. Downham too has had to modify the idea. Rather than a swap-shop of skills, it's become a voluntary service to put washers on leaking taps for the elderly.

If you're in the Ribble Valley, make a point of adding Downham to your collection of extraordinary villages. If you can find it, that is. Downham has the courage to stand by a principle, regardless of what others think. I like that. One day the new millennium might come knocking at its door, but so far, there's no sign of it – forgive the pun.

You'll see no signposts, no wires, no road markings and no television aerials in Downham.

ELECTRIC AVENUE

Drax, Yorkshire

On the one hand I was entranced by majestic curves of concrete rising seductively from the Yorkshire floodplain. On the other hand I was disappointed that Man, in his insatiable quest for energy, could dream up something so brutal. It takes your breath away.

Welcome to Drax, once a farming village in the Ouse valley but now host to the biggest coal-fired power station in Britain and the second biggest in Europe. It has twelve cooling towers, each of which could accommodate St. Paul's Cathedral, and an 850 foot chimney which is almost twice as high as the London Eye!

I have a love-hate relationship with power stations. When they're in full steam, they look from a distance like a huddle of old men smoking their pipes. But catch them at sunrise or sunset and they're as captivating as the pyramids. On the day I called, the shadows of billowing steam on the flanks of the Drax towers made me wish I'd brought my canvas and paints.

Why, I wondered, did the Central Electricity Generating Board inflict this sinister giant on little ol' Drax? And how did the villagers feel 40 years on? Was the power station friend or foe? Since many of them work at the plant or

Left: Britain's biggest power station: so ugly, it's almost beautiful.

have relatives who do, the reaction was mostly positive. Others shrugged their shoulders and confessed they didn't notice it any more. Power station – what power station? It's remarkable what you can get used to.

Dorothy Thompson, Chief Executive Officer of Drax Group Plc was full of enthusiasm. She has to be. Greenpeace are on her back. The trend is away from coal-fired stations. A million miles away. Carbon emissions from the plant probably exceed a year's worth of traffic on the M1. In its dirtiest coal-burning days, Drax was Western Europe's single biggest polluter. A dozen wind turbines on the eastern side of the village seem to say: 'Look this way folks. We're your future.' I'm no fan of wind turbines but coal surely has had its day. Dorothy nodded:

'We're switching more and more to bio-mass – wood from sustainable sources. Each pile has to be accurately labelled because we have to know the source. We have a generating capacity of 3,960 megawatts, ten times more than any other power station in the UK. We provide 7% of Britain's electricity. Our relationship with the village is very good. We called the power station Drax as a tribute to them.'

Britain's newest train service duly went into operation in December 2013, carrying 2,000 tonnes of timber offcut to be burned in the Drax furnaces. The Woodchip Express, commissioned and bought by the stock market-quoted power station, travels via the east coast ports of Hull, Immingham and Tyne in a set of 25 wagons, purpose-built in Nottinghamshire.

But let's go back. The CEGB built the station on the site of Drax Abbey, which was destroyed during the reign of Henry VIII. When work began in 1964, villagers didn't know what had hit them. Philip Roberts, an arable farmer who also owns Drax Livery, was at primary school:

'The place was transformed. Dozens of Scottish labourers from the disused shipyards moved into temporary accommodation. Sons and daughters of local farmers earned extra money driving heavy machinery because they were used to it. Drax came alive. We had a village store and a butcher's shop in those days. Business boomed for them and the pub.'

The pub's still there and so is the school, but Drax has no shops. Young professionals commute to Leeds or Hull. The rest of the village leans on the power station for its sporting and social requirements. Like it or not, it's a valuable institution.

The question remains though – why did the CEGB favour this part of Yorkshire when Ferrybridge and Eggborough power stations were more or less next door? The answer is coal. Mountains of it were on the doorstep. It came by rail from the deep mines of nearby Selby which outlived the Thatcher/Scargill era. Now, ironically, coal comes more cheaply from Russia, Colombia and the USA.

Though he has no connections with the plant, Philip Roberts has embraced it wholeheartedly. He's done a tour of the inner workings and even taken three lifts to the top of the chimney. From here, you can see beyond the Humber Bridge.

And the wind turbines? Ah yes, they were his idea. Philip got a private company to install them on his land. They belong to EDF who pay him a handsome rent for the privilege. Inevitably, a protest group did its best to put a spoke in the works, but he had the local MP and Selby District Council on his side. No problem. Lucrative farm diversification. The turbines are 60ft high with 20ft rotors. Some believe implicitly in them as an alternative energy source. Others, including me, think we're smothering the countryside with ugly, synthetic forests. For its part, the government's cutting back on green energy and committing itself to nuclear. But I've a feeling Drax is here to stay. As Eddie Grant might say, it really *is* Electric Avenue.

Drax is switching to burning timber off-cuts instead of coal.

SHINGLE-MINDED

Dungeness, Kent

'Dungeness is a magical place. When you visit, tread softly, for many choose to live here for the solitude and silence.'

So wrote Keith Collins in his preface to *Derek Jarman's Garden*, the last book written by the controversial author and filmmaker. Upon discovering in 1983 that he was HIV positive, Jarman bought an old fisherman's cottage facing the English Channel on this exposed stretch of earth – and created a striking garden of driftwood and alpines in the bleakest conditions imaginable.

Dungeness is blasted by force 14 winds in winter and roasted by what's described as 'Death Valley sun' in the summer. A touch melodramatic perhaps, but it's true there's no sunnier and no drier place in the UK. Jarman died in Prospect Cottage. It's empty now but it's still the first thing visitors come to see. As well-presented as it is, it prompts the thought: how the hell could anyone *live* there?

The stylish way to reach Dungeness is by steam train. A unique passenger service runs most days of most weeks. Among others, it has carried employees to and from Dungeness Nuclear Power Station. It still takes thirty or so local kids to school every morning. But a warning – you'll have to mind your head. It's built more like a toy train. On a clear blue September day, its tiny coaches brought scores of passengers across the marshes to New Romney before continuing south westwards towards the heart of this bizarre community. In doing so, the loco chugged through back gardens and past washing lines, before finally offering customers the strange panorama of a broad shingle landscape, speckled with stand-alone wood huts, boats in dry dock and Victorian railway carriages converted into homes. This is Dungeness.

Officially, it's a desert. The largest shingle desert in the world. But it's also a village. Admittedly, it lacks some of the essential prerequisites of a village. There's no post office, no church and no village hall. Neither does it have a parish council. The Dungeness Trust which

Dungeness village is a curious collection of wooden huts sprinkled on the world's largest shingle desert.

runs it as a private estate, prefers to call it 'a community'. What it *does* have is a lifeboat station, an art gallery, a hut selling the freshest fish in Europe and 82 hardy souls hunkered down in a variety of scattered abodes. Sounds like a village to me.

'Pretty' would be stretching a point. 'Arresting' is a better description. The shingle's broken up by scruffy outcrops of gorse. There are poles, wires and pylons everywhere. Then there's the iron grey lump that is Dungeness Nuclear Power Station. Two reactors fused into one. Dungeness A is in the lengthy process of being decommissioned; Dungeness B still has fifteen years to go. Confronted by this kaleidoscope of wilderness and industrialisation, I began to understand the love/hate relationship people have with this place. A relative of mine who belongs in the first category, was thrilled to hear that I'd selected Dungeness for inclusion in the book.

'Fantastic!' she cried, 'It's one of my favourite places. I'll buy you the best fish and chips you'll ever taste.'

How could I turn that down? Dungeness is only thirty minutes from where she lives. She and her late husband were regular visitors. They'd picnic on the 'beach'. They'd buy fish. I invited her to be my guide. Our tiny train pulled up at Dungeness station and the scene that greeted us was almost unreal. At the station café, two dozen schoolgirls chatted animatedly. They were on a geography field trip.

A second group of girls had made the long climb to the top of a disused lighthouse and were calling from its circular balcony. A hundred yards beyond, four helmeted workmen clambered over the roof of Dungeness A, untroubled by the 'bomb' they were sitting on.

Meanwhile, a small band of drinkers enjoyed the sun outside the *Britannia Inn*. No-one took any notice of anyone else, as though station, café, lighthouse, pub and plutonium were natural bedfellows. It's the most extraordinary of village hubs.

From the lighthouse you can see how layers of shingle have been washed ashore over hundreds of years to create this unique desert. The 'beach' is expanding by a metre a year, pushing the sea further and further away. My relative observed that Dungeness was more crowded than the last time she called. There were more huts, more boats and more people. For all that, we failed to find anyone at home. The huts were locked up. Nothing indigenous moved across the landscape. Where did the gentlefolk of Dungeness go in the daytime?

The mystery's part explained by the fact that most of the huts are holiday lets. Even the parish church had been converted for that purpose. The second point is that Dungeness folk famously covet their privacy. I suppose they wouldn't live here otherwise. Many a reporter and cameramen has been drummed out of the place. Tourists who stray off the beaten track have been known to get a mouthful.

We had no such problem with Norman Sands who works for Romney, Hythe and Dymchurch Railway, the private limited company which operates this 15-inch gauge train service. The locomotive's only four feet high. The carriages hold a maximum of four people each. There's no standing room. But the railway does more business now than at any time since it was built as a rich man's toy in 1927. In his spare time, Norman was so moved by Dungeness that he wrote a book about it. He first discovered it on a family holiday when he was six years old. It has made an indelible impression. Taking a deep breath, he said:

'The air's so good. And it's so quiet here. [The schoolgirls had gone.] This is what they mean by the expression 'a deafening silence.' I've experienced nothing like it since hot-air ballooning in Kenya.'

So what was the magic of Dungeness?

'Hard to pinpoint. It's a strange but unique environment in Britain. You either love it or hate it. It's a Site of Special Scientific Interest because of the birds and the rare plant life. That means it's unspoilt: you can't interfere with anything. I wanted to live here once but my wife refused. Dungenesss is too bleak for her. Artists and photographers are attracted by the light and the combination of fishing boats and tumbledown shacks. But

Above left: Derek Jarman bought this fisherman's cottage to escape the rat-race. Above right: The miniature steam railway once carried workers to the nuclear plant.

living here's another matter. With hindsight I'm glad we didn't. There's no *real* community any more. The days when womenfolk winched fishing boats up the shingle for their partners have gone.'

Norman pointed to a small blue building in the middle distance:

'You must call in there. That's the Fish Hut. The owner goes fishing at night and sells his catch the next morning. You'll get nothing fresher. Eating fish that has only been out of the water for an hour is a different sensation. And he cooks fabulous cod baps.'

We headed towards the hut on shingle paths between the grasses, only to find that it too was deserted. What else could you expect in a desert? Presumably the fisherman had sold his catch and gone. At least my

Below: Still sinister even though it's out-of-action: the nuclear plant is being decommissioned.

relative was able to show me another of Dungeness's oddities – a building clad, top-to-toe, in black rubber. Was it protection against extreme weather or nuclear fall-out? Or maybe the designer was a rubber fetishist? No-one seems to be sure, but it's a pretty depressing sight. By way of contrast, a dazzling chrome caravan is parked outside. There's no accounting for taste. I knocked at the door. No-one was in.

The area has a deceptively random feel. Huts disappear into the distance; cars are left willy-nilly beside a solitary highway. There are no fences or gates – no boundaries except the horizon. You wonder whether anyone's keeping a check on all of this. What are the limits? What are the rules? As it turns out, Dungeness is the most tightly designated landscape in Britain, both from a construction and environmental point of view. Between them, Natural England, the RSPB and Shepway District Council stop you putting a single toe in the wrong place. You need permission to blow your nose.

There's an outright ban on new homes. The only hope of living here is to pay around £250,000 for a footprint. That's if someone want to sell. Much to the residents' annoyance, speculators are allowed to demolish ancient wooden houses and rebuild them in modern materials. The rubber house was the first example. As I write, there are four such projects underway.

You can walk for miles in/on Dungeness but it's tough going when you stray off the boardwalks. We took the easier option and *drove* to the far side of the village in search of the world class fish and chips I'd been promised. We eventually landed at *The Pilot Inn*. The chips were plump and fleshy, the peas were mushy and the fish was line-caught that very day. The best I'd ever tasted? They bore comparison with a fish and chip supper I once enjoyed in Grimsby – probably the highest praise you can get. Only the pot of tea and a plate of bread-and-butter were missing.

Even from here, the Magnox reactors of Dungeness A still dominated the skyline. In the other direction, seagulls whirled over an endless stretch of shingle which glittered in the sun until it met with the bluest of blue skies. Dungeness could grow on me.

The shingle beach grows bigger every day.

GOOD AFTERNOON CONSTABLE

East Bergholt, Suffolk

Flatford Mill is so English you could spread it on your crumpets. Ducks and geese dip their heads in a millpond overhung with ash trees and edged with Queen Anne's lace (cow parsley). And there stands Willy Lott's cottage, immortalised in John Constable's most famous painting, The Haywain. Only the trees have changed in two centuries.

I'd followed the instructions and walked to the exact spot where Constable stood to paint his masterpiece. Willy Lott's cottage now accommodates art students who flock to the Mill hoping that some of the painter's genius rubs off. Willy was a farmer who only spent four nights away from his cottage in his 80-year life. Fame came indirectly and posthumously.

My thoughts were interrupted by the crunch of wheels on gravel as a minibus pulled up behind me. Out poured a group of Dutch youngsters who'd come to Flatford to study 'England and Englishness'. But of course! Constable would have felt vindicated. He was always preaching the beauties of Suffolk – the Stour valley in particular. Even after moving to London, he returned to Flatford for his holidays each summer. This is what he wrote to his great friend John Fisher in 1821:

'The sound of water escaping from mill dams…willows, old rotten banks, slimy posts and brickwork…. I love such things. As long as I do paint I shall never cease to paint such places.'

Although it's a hamlet in its own right, Flatford doesn't technically exist in local government terms. It's part of East Bergholt, a pastel-coloured village where Constable was born and raised. The whole area, including the neighbouring village of Dedham, is known as Constable Country. It was the first geographical area to be

Déjà vu! Willy Lott's cottage at Flatford, a scene barely changed since John Constable sat here in 1821 and painted The Hay Wain.

It's easy to see why John Constable adored his native Suffolk and Flatford Mill (above) in particular. His father once owned it.

named after an artist. Suffolk's answer to Shakespeare Country, you might say. Public pilgrimages began in the late 1800s when Thomas Cook & Son added 'A visit to Constable Country' to its list of tours. Well-heeled Europeans and Americans lapped it up. It's a curious thing that Constable was appreciated abroad – in Paris to be precise – before he was fully recognised in his own country. The Great Eastern Railway also laid on coaches at Colchester to meet passengers off the London train and drive them to Flatford.

There was no shortage of takers for the weekend course I subscribed to. In fact, all the rooms at Flatford Mill and Willy Lott's Cottage were booked. East Bergholt guesthouses told me there were 'no vacancies'. Not bad for the middle of May. I had to book in at Dedham, a 20-minute walk along the river Stour, or half an hour by rowboat. Constable went to school at Dedham, a magnificent Georgian village just across the border in Essex. It makes nonsense of the common preconception that Essex is a county to avoid. Art is very much in the air here too. My guesthouse, The Fountain at Dedham Hall also runs painting holidays throughout the year. I was lucky to get a bed. Twenty five water-colourists arrived the day I checked out.

Fortunately, the battalions of amateur painters spread themselves throughout the Stour valley, otherwise you wouldn't move for easels. There's a wealth of subject matter, from the boatyards of Mistley and Manningtree to the half-timbered houses of Dedham and the buttercup meadows of East Bergholt. The majority, however, are drawn to Flatford at some point in their stay. It is, inevitably, a little twee these days, with a National Trust tearoom and shop next to the boat-hire barn – but no less captivating.

The Mill was once owned by Constable's father, Golding, a prosperous corn merchant who also had a shipping operation in Mistley. By the late 1920s Flatford Mill had lost its millstone and was in bad shape. An Ipswich benefactor, Thomas Parkington bought the estate and presented it to the nation on his death as a tribute to John Constable. The National Trust leased the Mill to the Field Studies Council in 1946 – and the rest is history. I have no idea how many budding Constables have walked through its period doors since then, but few of them can have failed to be uplifted by the mood it creates. Here's Constable's description:

'The beauty of the surrounding scenery, its gentle declivities, its luxuriant meadow flats sprinkled with flocks and herds, its well cultivated uplands, its woods and rivers with numerous scattered villages and churches, farms and picturesque cottages, all impart to this particular spot an amenity and elegance hardly anywhere else to be found.'

I'm sure our Dutch visitors would agree. As I left, they were tucking into Bakewell tart – another essential element of 'England and Englishness.' But that's another story.

Rowing up the river Stour from Dedham to Flatford Mill is a popular pastime.

BACK TO THE SIXTIES

Eel Pie Island, Middlesex

You don't have to be left field to live on Eel Pie Island, but it's marginally preferable. This is more than a village. It's a way of life. Outsiders are tolerated rather than encouraged. The first sign to greet you states: 'Private Island. No Thoroughfare. No access to the river. No cycling'. Charming!

Thirty five yards of river Thames and a footbridge make a heck of a difference. On one side, the urban cacophony of Twickenham; on the other, the rustic calm of a bohemian community clinging to a rocky outcrop. The name 'Eel Pie' derives from the lunches offered to Victorian day-trippers cruising the river. They were reliving the culinary habits of Henry VIII who regularly stopped off for bellyfuls of eel pie on his way to Hampton Court Palace. Alas, eels became a rarity as the Thames grew dirtier and, despite the clean-up in recent years, the pies are history.

But the name survives and so does the spirit of Eel Pie Island. Technically, it's part of Twickenham

Separated from Twickenham by a small stretch of water and a little bridge – but worlds apart.

Borough Council. In reality, you step into a different world once you cross the bridge. The tidal waters of the Thames have virtually carved a small independent state. Passports may be just around the corner. As far as I can work out, there are three footpaths across the island, all of them lined with flowering shrubs and overhung with mature trees. I followed the main thoroughfare (about 100 yards long) and was visually assaulted by a wardrobe of women's clothing suspended from the fence on hangers. Nice. A handwritten poster said 'All Free'. Fair enough. Next came a white building with a red tin roof, called The Loveshack. It carried a notice saying: 'thank you for reading this notice.' Typical. Then came a corrugated tin house painted green and decorated with old adverts for Punch magazine and HMV. A sign on the gate warned of a forty shillings penalty for 'omitting to fasten it.' See what I mean by left field?

Apart from the intermittent rumble of Heathrow jets, Eel Pie felt peaceful. Where *was* everyone? This was in marked contrast to the 1960s when Britain's flower-power youth decamped here to see the top bands perform at Eel Pie Island Hotel. They included The Rolling Stones, The Who, The Yardbirds and David Bowie. Before that, the hotel was a major jazz emporium, attracting ferryloads of enthusiasts who came to dance and find a mate. The hotel burned down in 1976 while it was being demolished. In its less glorious years, the building was claimed by squatters who turned it into a drugs den.

My footpath hit the buffers. In front of me, the steel walls of Eel Pie Island Slipway Ltd. whose telephone number still carried the old 01 prefix for London. I knew from previous experience that a gentle push on the wicket gate would let me through. Access is normally restricted to islanders who live on the far side of the boatyard but no-one seemed to mind. A battered old tanker was in dry dock awaiting a refit and a woman with a paintbrush was freshening up the plimsoll line on her houseboat. Was I trespassing? A mechanic nodded his tacit approval as I passed through the yard. Visitors were obviously a rare occurrence. He told me he would never consider leaving the island and he cast a dismissive glance over his shoulder towards Twickenham saying:

'I hate going there. Too many people.'

The alley opened into a chaotic but charming collection of boating paraphernalia and upturned vessels converted into artists' studios. A skeleton in a cage hung on a doorway; a rusting metal press gathered spiders; a technicolour line of washing dried in the hot sun. There was a faint but delicious aroma of dhal.

Eel Pie Island has 26 resident artists, jewellers and ceramicists who open their studios to the public twice a year. Sarah Hubacher, a silk screen printer, was racing against deadlines to produce three six-foot long seascapes. Se told me:

'I came here to work but I wish I'd moved in permanently. Such a great atmosphere.'

But Sarah's artistic neighbour, Lee Campbell, had a different take on Eel Pie Island:

'I couldn't cope with the island mentality if I lived here. It's claustrophobic. There's no escape.'

She put the finishing touches to a view from Richmond Hill – a subject she has painted scores of times in several different ways. It was like watching Cézanne paint Mont Sainte-Victoire again and again. Sarah's customers don't seem to tire of it so why not?

Top: Sarah Hubacher, silk screen printer
Middle: 'The island was a brothel,' says Trevor Baylis.
Bottom: House names are thoroughly in-keeping.

I'd come to a dead end. There's no terrestrial access to the nature reserve which separates the artists' commune from the far side of the Thames, so I retraced my steps along the main path. My next destination was Henry Harrison's office complex which inflamed the islanders when he proposed it ten years ago. He was ordered to design the offices in the same style as the artists' workshops they replaced. The various shacks and

Richmond Yacht Club has been based on Eel Pie Island since 1962, and houses the island's other bar.

A tin house with 1950s adverts fits perfectly into the landscape.

converted boats burned down when a firework strayed into their midst. I don't think Henry's done a bad job to be honest. At least the complex brings much-needed business to the island.

There's a right turn to Twickenham Rowing Club, founded in 1860, making it one of the oldest in the country. It houses one of two bars on Eel Pie Island but, disappointingly, the gate was locked. Eel Pie houses are a mixture of glorified shacks, 1970s shoeboxes and brand new manifestations. None of them would win design awards. They either front directly onto the path or are accessed along private walkways. There are fifty houses in all, accommodating a population of around 120. If you value privacy, this is not the place for you.

I eventually found what I was looking for. A house called The Haven, belonging to the celebrated inventor, Trevor Baylis. He first hit the headlines when he introduced wind-up radios to Aids sufferers in Africa who had no access to electricity. He was awarded the OBE, featured in a *Tomorrow's World* programme and starred in *This is Your Life*. However, unlike Percy Shaw, the man who invented cats' eyes, Trevor's genius failed to make him a million. He's philosophical about it:

'People found a way around the patenting laws and copied my idea. It's sod's law. Percy just happened to see a cat's eyes glowing as it came towards him. If the cat had been going the other way, he'd have invented the pencil sharpener!'

Trevor's 76 now. He's been a physical training instructor, a circus entertainer and a stuntman for Peter Cook and Dudley Moore. One performance in Berlin earned him £17,000 in 1970. He immediately bought a plot of land on the quieter side of Eel Pie Island and had a house built overlooking the water. We sat on his elevated patio watching canoeists paddle by. The patio's covered in synthetic grass with tubs of plastic flowers acting as

NOTICE
THANK YOU
FOR NOTICING THIS
NEW NOTICE

a safety barrier against a fifteen feet drop into the Thames. An extra feature is the open top sports car he built himself but which never hit the road. It looks curious on a patio – but then this is Eel Pie Island. Trevor talked fondly about his 'corner of paradise':

'It's a village like villages used to be. We all look after each other. Six or seven people have a key to my place. When I'm not here, they can use the lathe. '

Is he an ageing hippie?

'I suppose so. You had to be to live here. I first came as young man to enjoy the music – and to get my leg over. The girls were worse than the boys. The island was a brothel. The dance floor was like a trampoline. I never married. Didn't need to. Marriage isn't a word, it's a sentence!'

He's good at the one-liners. A born entertainer as well as an inventor. I can't imagine him living anywhere but Eel Pie Island.

Heading back to the footbridge, I wondered where the islanders kept their cars. Perhaps they don't need them. Twickenham main line station's only half a mile away. You're at Waterloo in twenty minutes. The far bank was seething with mothers and children enjoying the school holidays. They probably didn't give a thought to the funny place across the river, let alone venture across the bridge. Sometimes you need waders to get across. The river spills over the sidewalk, leaving the approach to the bridge under two feet of water. It was worse before the Thames barrier.

I crossed back to civilisation as Twickenham knows it with the Great Inventor's parting words in my head:

'Tell 'em we islanders are a special breed, but we *do* occasionally have time for the common folk on the mainland!'

Left: Boat repairs are big business on Eel Pie Island today.

THIRSTY WORK

Elan Village, Powys

I threaded my way through the Cambrian Mountains in search of a titanic piece of engineering. It was eerie. Nothing else moved in this sparsely populated wilderness. Right on cue, the heavens opened. Although this would seriously dilute my photo opportunities, it was only to be expected.

Rain was the point of the story. Seventy inches of it fall in mid-Wales each year, which is why Birmingham chose to build its reservoirs here. This is what I'd come to see – the UK's most dramatic reservoir complex and an accompanying village, created out of nothing, to house 1,500 navvies. The navvies are long gone, but the village remains, albeit in a much-changed form.

Thanks to their efforts over a rigorous twelve year period, millions of gallons of drinking water travel 72 miles from Rhayader to Birmingham every day. Without it, England's second city would dry up. The fact that

Above: Craig Goch Dam. A village was created for the 1,500 navvies working on Britain's biggest reservoir project.

the water is propelled by gravity alone is a tribute to a genius called James Mansergh who designed the Elan Valley Project in 1893. The idea came from Birmingham Corporation, responding nervously to this warning from the chairman of its Water Committee:

> 'Gentlemen, there has been yet another outbreak of smallpox and diarrhoea in our city. We need pure water. Remember, fellow councillors, cleanliness is next to Godliness.' (1880)

… And scooping holes out of solid rock is next to impossible. Especially without a JCB. But they did it. The navvies were joined by skilled masons who hand-faced thousands of stone blocks in the dam walls with hammer and chisel. The finished article is breathtaking. Walkers, mountain bikers and fishermen lose themselves in this vast terrain. A flight of five reservoirs climbs higher and higher into the mountains. The views are Alpine; the reflections mirror-like. Almost everyone benefitted from the project. In total, some five thousand men gained employment, Birmingham's burgeoning population was saved from cholera, typhoid and smallpox and Wales was gifted the double whammy of a magnificent new landscape and a tourist attraction to boost the economy.

However, most tourists overlook a hamlet called Elan Village which nestles up against a 125 foot–high dam, holding back enough water to deluge the entire valley. The village is unique. It was grafted onto a barren landscape to accommodate the workforce. Each house was built of rough, tarred wood. Although quickly thrown together, it included a hospital, a school, a community centre, a bath house, a post office and a church – by no means your average shanty town.

Birmingham Corporation had compulsorily purchased 71 square miles of Wales and, not without local opposition, submerged two manor houses, several farms and a church to achieve its objective. One hundred or so people were forced to leave the valley. Only landowners were compensated.

The wind howled, the rain drummed against my windscreen and the light began to fade. Well, it *was* December. Through the gloom, I caught a glimpse of water spraying into the air halfway up a mountain. An illusion? No, it was the gale whipping up a frenzy on Caban Coch reservoir. A warden at the visitor centre assured me this was mild compared with the 80 mph storms they'd endured a few days earlier. There were four-foot waves on the reservoirs! Who would choose to live in this cold, dark, wet place, scenic though it was.

The wooden homes of the workers were dismantled and Elan was rebuilt as a model village.

The navvies had no choice, but now?

Visibility had almost gone so I decided to leave the village until tomorrow and booked in at a hotel on the outskirts of Rhayader. It's a quaint little town with a clock tower and a seemingly endless supply of pubs. When the navvies were here, they had *thirteen* alehouses to choose from. It's believed to be a British record. Nevertheless, the Corporation discouraged excessive drinking among its employees and enforced a strict code of conduct. For security reasons, they built Elan Village on the far side of the tumbling river Elan. Anyone entering or leaving had to cross a wire suspension bridge and satisfy the gatekeeper that they were legitimate.

It was still raining the next morning as I drove over an adjoining bridge to see how Elan Village had changed since those pioneering days. The first thing to tell you is that it's no longer made of wood. Timber town was dismantled once the reservoirs were completed. In its place, Birmingham Corporation designed a 'model village' to serve as a permanent reminder of the remarkable past. It's an art-deco hamlet consisting of twelve houses, an estate office and a business training centre where the school used to be. A line of stone-built semis with sizeable garden plots stand rather forlornly on a narrow strip of land between the river and the escarpment. Residents are bereft of services. There's no shop, no school, no church, no public house, and not even a village hall. Two rusty goal frames lean at different angles on a piece of scrub that once passed as a football pitch. On a wet Sunday in December, Elan Village was distinctly short of cheer.

Acting on the advice of Max Walker, a warden employed by Welsh Water, I knocked at number 8 and was met by a slightly bemused couple, Reg and Mary Williams. Mary was in the process of making sausage rolls for the Christmas fair and basting a pheasant for Sunday lunch. Her husband's job brought them here 47 years ago.

Reg was a water bailiff responsible for patrolling the dams, supervising the fishing and ejecting campers. He explained:

'I was the only bailiff here. It's funny when you look back. The reservoirs could be dangerous in bad weather but we didn't even have life jackets in those days. I couldn't swim either!'

The couple pay a weekly rent of £100 to the estate, once owned by Birmingham Corporation, then Severn Trent, but now Welsh Water – or a combination of the two. Even the tenants aren't sure of their landlord's identity. At any rate, number 8 is home for the Williams for as long as they wish. They seemed happy enough, but I wanted to know whether Elan Village was a proper community or just a relic? Mary, a former school-teacher, replied:

'I know what you mean. It's a bit quiet but we do have one or two social events and a big bonfire on November 5th. Most of the residents are retired but a couple still work on the estate. This is a cold valley. They can't insulate the houses because there aren't any cavity walls.'

Villagers have access to a church but it's a mile away at Nantgwyllt and stands in spooky isolation among the Scots pines on high ground overlooking one of the dams. The church was built by the Corporation in the early 1900s to replace the one they flooded. There are no houses around it. Worshippers gather once a month for services by gas lamp.

Reg and Mary tried to buy their house from the estate. They even enlisted the support of their local MP. The answer was 'no'. Welsh Water/ Severn Trent wanted to keep the village just as it was. Nevertheless, three houses *are* privately owned. One of them, a smart three-bed semi at the end of the row, had been on the market for more than two years and was still unsold. The asking price dropped from £200,000 to £185,000. Model village or no, people aren't queuing up to live in Elan. What could be putting them off, apart from the cold?'

A reminder of the men who toiled in awful conditions to provide Birmingham with clean water.

'Gnats,' said Mary without hesitation. 'We're infested with them in summer. They breed on the reservoirs. We stay indoors during the day and shut the windows at night.'

The folks at number 7 were huddled around a log fire. Sunday was rest day for John Edwards. He's usually mending fences and herding sheep on the estate. After 24 years in Australia, his English wife, Linda finds the cold and damp a problem. But she's fond of the valley and its marvellous wildlife. While otters struggle to establish themselves across the border in England, Elan villagers are almost falling over them! The air's full of buzzards and peregrines. Linda told me:

It's a brooding kind of village, overshadowed by misty mountains.

'When we first came here in 1993, there was a beautiful avenue of horse chestnuts along the riverbank. At blossom time, visitors would put up their deckchairs at the water's edge as though it was a beach. The trees became diseased so they had to be cut down. We miss them.'

Back in the visitor centre, I noticed several sightings of stoats and otters chalked on the blackboard. Max Walker told me he recently watched a weasel encircle and mesmerise a rabbit for several minutes. The rabbit squealed in panic but was rooted to the spot. Eventually the weasel went for the jugular, capturing a prey four or five times its own size.

'An incredible sight,' he said. 'Even I was mesmerised.'

As a boy, Max couldn't wait to get out of London. He left school at 16, bound for a sheep station at Invercargill on the south island of New Zealand. Before he set sail, his prospective employer died, leaving Max to find an alternative escape route. At random, he chose Radnorshire (now Powys) although he'd never heard of the place. He began rounding up sheep and has been in the Elan valley ever since. Why?

'I love it. It gets to you.'

Although the village and the reservoirs are artificial, they fit into the landscape. In fact, the reservoirs enhance it. And when all's said and done, Man dug the holes but he needed Nature to fill them up.

THE ULTIMATE SACRIFICE

Eyam, Derbyshire

Maria Banks stepped out of her front door to bring in the milk. She'd removed her curlers and changed out of her dressing gown and slippers. Mrs Banks has to look the part. She never knows who's watching. Visitors are drawn to Eyam at all times of year and all times of day. They all make a beeline for Maria's cottage. Although it hasn't been in the headlines for more than three hundred years, they can't resist hearing the story again – and again.

As it turned out this particular morning, Maria needn't have worried. There was no-one on the street. Her milk duties went unobserved. But she warned:

'You've got to be careful living here. I'm an unofficial tour guide, always on parade. People expect me to be suitably dressed.'

Her address might be a deterrent to some, but to most it has an irresistibly ghoulish appeal – 2, Plague Cottages, Main Street, Eyam. Mail doesn't exactly cascade through her letterbox. Postmen are reluctant to get too close. Chloe Holmes, the receptionist at Eyam Museum, confessed that *she* couldn't live in the cottage. She knows too much about it. And yet aspiring tenants usually have to join the waiting list.

I'd better explain. Number 2 Plague Cottages is where Bubonic Plague started in 1665. A father, his assistant and his two stepsons perished in quick succession. It was by pure chance that Eyam became enmeshed in an epidemic mostly confined to London. The father, Alexander Hardwick, was a tailor. He ordered a consignment of cloth from the capital. It arrived damp and smelling foul. The tailor's assistant, George Viccars spread the material in front of the fire to dry out. Fatal. It released a small swarm of fleas which had travelled with the cloth. Stirred by the heat, they started to feed – not on their usual source, the black rat, but on George. He was dead within days. Four more people in neighbouring cottages died soon afterwards. Bubonic Plague was established. Before it subsided fourteen months later, it would kill 260 villagers.

Left: Eyam will always be known as 'the plague village'.

Maria Banks' dream was to live in No.2 Plague Cottages

THE HAWKSWORTH FAMILY

Peter, the 3rd victim, died on the 23rd September 1665. Humphrey, aged 15 months, their son, died on 17th October 1665. Jane was the sole survivor in the household. All together, including her inlaws, she lost 25 relatives.

There are reminders everywhere of the village's sacrifice.

Maria has recounted the story a thousand times. She tells tourists that a mysterious hand strokes her hair in the dead of night; that she hears frequent sobbing and that a child sometimes materialises at her bedroom door before dematerialising just as quickly. Oh, and yes, her electric toothbrush occasionally switches itself on. Visitors shudders. Maria smiles. When you've waited 45 years for your dream home, a few ghosts won't put you off. They come with the territory. She said:

'I was open minded about ghosts when I signed the tenancy in 2007. I believe in them now!'

The experience has actually broadened her life. The doughty Mrs Banks has a new hobby. A paranormal investigation team from Stockport called Club Zero offered her automatic membership. Maria seized the chance:

'I've been on a couple of investigations with them, one at Eyam Museum. We use sound recordings and night vision cameras to eliminate the normal before isolating the paranormal. It's exciting.'

What is it they say about ill winds? It goes further. Eyam's economy is built around the plague. The catastrophe of 1665-6 is the village's tourist industry today. This former lead mining village was buzzing with people when I arrived. Café-goers lunched outside on a cold Saturday in December because the indoor tables were spoken for. Cyclists propped their bikes up against the café wall as if to say: 'We must take a close look at this place.' In the meantime, amateur photographers snapped away at Maria's cottage and at the plaque in her front garden. It confirms the death toll at number 2 Main Street. Only the tailor's wife survived, but she lost 13 relatives.

It may sound callous but with the exception of the boarded-up family butcher, George Siddall & Daughters, Eyam is profiting from its macabre place in history. The Lord of the Manor, Robert Wright, whose ancestors bought the estate shortly before the plague, conceded:

Eyam Hall was built six years after the plague ended. The Lord of the Manor grew rich on lead mining.

'Whether you like it or not, the plague brings money.'

The seventeenth-century Wrights were attracted to the village by its lead mining tradition. The mines boosted the family coffers but shortened the lives of the men who worked in them. Lead poisoning was an unknown hazard in those days. As far as Robert Wright can tell, none of his ancestors died in the plague. Their Jacobean manor, Eyam Hall was built six years later. Robert and his wife Nicola lived there for most of their married life but eventually found it too expensive and unwieldy. They handed it over to the National Trust. It too has become a commercial success.

The Hancocke family graves. Six children and their father died within a week.

I wouldn't call Eyam especially pretty but it occupies a prime location in the magnificent Derbyshire Dales. This is *real* country living. Traffic stops for twenty minutes while a shepherdess walks her flock down the hill to the lower pastures. Nobody minds. She waves thank you and we wave back. It's a pleasant diversion. Chatsworth House, the most visited stately home outside the London area, is a hop, skip and jump away. I once hired the Duchess of Devonshire as a TV presenter on our countryside programme. She was a natural. Her predecessors had food parcels and medicines delivered to the besieged village. The parcels were left on a standing stone a mile out of the village.

Although gripped by the plague, Eyam agreed to stand firm and face the consequences alone rather than flee and allow the infection to spread. It amounted to communal suicide. All they could do was sit in their homes and wait for death. According to legend, only two villagers, both women, defied the curfew. One fled to Tideswell but was immediately stoned out of town. Some of these details have been contested over the centuries, not least by local historian, Fran Clifford.

All the museum exhibits are based on her research. Swimming in an ocean of speculation, guesswork and rumour, Fran and her husband set about putting the record straight. Some stories, such as the woman who fled to Tideswell, have been impossible to verify or discount. Said Fran:

'All we've done is put flesh on the bones. There was plenty of ignorance. I remember schoolchildren asking whether any animals died during the plague. A simple question but no-one knew the answer. We still don't. The early reports claimed that only 83 villagers survived. Nonsense. Out of a population of eight hundred, 540 survived.'

What's *incontestable* is that the vicar, William Mompesson played a leading role in Eyam's unique stoicism. It was his idea to isolate the village. He closed the church to avoid indoor gatherings and stood on a rock pulpit to preach to grief-stricken villagers in an outdoor amphitheatre called Cucklett Delph. The services are re-enacted every year during the Eyam festival. It's not quite on the scale of the Oberammergau Passion Play, but it's a big event nonetheless.

The Reverend Mompesson also instructed villagers to bury their own dead. He and his wife led the heroic fight against Bubonic Plague before Mrs Mompesson eventually succumbed. The vicar lived on. His impressive figure adorns one of the church windows.

I took a walk out of the village to the Riley Graves, a sombre monument standing alone in the middle of a field high above the village. Enclosed within a circular dry-stone wall are the graves of the Hancocke family – six children and their father who died within a week of each other. There's no church, just a small cemetery on an exposed hillside. They're called the Riley Graves because the ground was part of Riley's farm. The Hancocke's cottage is no longer there. A party of scouts were leaving the monument as I arrived. They were unusually quiet. The graves have that effect. For a few moments, you're divorced from the reality of 21st century Eyam and catapulted back to the time when fear, suspicion and death stalked the Peak. Mrs Hancocke was the only member of the family to survive. She buried her husband and all of the children before escaping in the most appalling state to stay with a relative in Sheffield. That could have torpedoed the whole exercise. Fortunately, Mrs Hancocke wasn't carrying the disease.

Below: William Hancocke's wife buried her husband and children then broke the village's self-imposed pledge to stay put when she fled to Sheffield.

Nicola Wright, a Surrey girl who married into the family and has immersed herself in a community and a landscape she adores observed that what happened at Eyam could never happen today. She said:

'This is still a wonderful, caring community but self-sacrifice is not on anyone's agenda here or anywhere else.'

So what persuaded 800 people lay down their lives for the greater good. Was it as straightforward as self sacrifice?

'To a degree,' said Nicola, 'but we must remember that these were frightened people. They probably believed they were being punished for their sins. They'd do anything the church told them to.'

She and her husband, a retired solicitor, own twelve properties and 200 acres of farmland. Their houses include the plague cottages. There's rarely a shortage of people wanting to rent them. Maria Banks is one of their favourite tenants. Her enthusiasm is more contagious than Bubonic Plague itself. It dates back to a long-standing passion for Eyam and its tragic tale. You could call it obsession. Here's how it began:

'I came on a school trip when I was nine years old. The Eyam story gripped me. I stood outside number 2 Plague Cottages and said to myself: 'I'm going to live here one day.' It took me more than 40 years, but I've done it! I had no qualms about living in a house where so many people died. In fact, it brought me close to them.'

When someone tipped her off that Plague Cottage might be available, she fired up her trike (a three-wheeled motorbike) and headed for the Dales – a forty minute ride from Borrowash where she lived. Builders working on the cottage confirmed that it *was* coming up for rent. Six months later, she had the keys in her hands.

'I felt I belonged here. They'll have to carry me out in a box.'

Not in dressing gown and slippers, I'll wager. She has more style than that.

Left: the plague cottages have become highly sought-after homes.

HIGHEST VILLAGE IN BRITAIN

Flash, Staffordshire

You'd expect it to be in the Grampians or Snowdonia. At least the Pennines. But no, Britain's highest village is officially in Staffordshire Moorlands, a treeless and often daunting part of the Peak District between the bric-a-brac capital of Leek and the spa town of Buxton, itself the highest *town* in Britain.

I'm talking about Flash, a village where life has seldom been easy but people are as solid as the millstone grit that underpins them. The village sign says it's 1518 feet above sea level. Actually it's 40 feet higher, about which more in a moment. Suffice to say, looking down from the loftiest perch in the UK is important to Flash. It needs a USP.

Derbyshire is the glamour side of the Peak. Staffordshire is less showy, grittier, poorer. I'm standing on the southern slopes of Axe Head Moor, so untamed it could be the Tibetan plateau. The views are breathtaking and uninterrupted. Forests were cut down centuries ago to produce pit props for the mines. Traditionally in Flash, husbands farmed, chiselled coal or worked in the quarry. Wives made buttons at home in the evening.

Sheep farming continues today but on a much smaller scale. Leek and Macclesfield are the job centres. If you're young, you've probably left. There's nothing to keep you. The primary school closed on New Year's Day 2013. They were down to three pupils. One of the village stalwarts, Eddie Kidd who farms with his two sons, lamented:

'Kids used to be everywhere. Now you don't see them. That can only mean one thing – the village is dying.'

Left: Long before its altitude fame, Flash was notorious for its counterfeit coins.

The fact that Flash has survived abject poverty over the centuries makes me think it'll battle through. They only disbanded the village charity in 1995. It was known as The Old Teapot Club – real name, Flash Royal Union Society. Villagers each contributed one pound a year. The charity looked after the sick and needy and also contributed towards funeral costs. It came to an end when Robert Maxwell's shenanigans with the Daily Mirror Pension Fund forced the government to change the rules about friendly societies. The Old Teapot Club couldn't afford the legislation. Nevertheless, it continues as a social club. The annual Teapot Club church service was due the very week I called.

Poverty may well explain Flash's infamous reputation for counterfeit money. Legend says that in the early 1900s, forgers used button-making machines to produce fake coins. 'Flash money' was then exchanged at Three Shires Head, a nearby landmark where Staffordshire, Derbyshire and Cheshire meet. Local historian Margaret Parker, who lives in the last button-maker's house, confirms that counterfeit coins *were* in circulation but can't find any proof that they were forged in Flash.

She also casts doubt on rumours of cannibalism in the parish. Apparently a mother and daughter team were renowned for their meat pies at Leek market until a traveller who stayed at their bed and breakfast establishment overheard them talking about human bodies in the oven and shopped them to the local constabulary. The next time you buy a meat pie in Leek, it might be worth glancing at the ingredients label!

And so to the altitude question. For years, the village of Wanlockhead in Dumfries and Galloway had tried to steal Flash's thunder as the highest settlement in Britain. It claimed to measure 1,531 feet above sea level, against Flash's 1,518. Imagine the excitement when we turned up with a camera crew, a production team and a group of geo-physicists wielding GPS equipment to prove (or disprove) once and for all that Flash was top dog. By 'we' I mean my independent television company on behalf of BBC's 'The One Show'. Our reporter was the Iron Lady's daughter, Carol Thatcher.

In the interests of fairness, we sent a similar squad to Wanlockhead. The upshot was that Flash actually gained 40 feet and Wanlockhead was downgraded to 1,456. Furious Scotsmen went home with their tails between their legs. By contrast, Flash soared in everyone's estimation. The publicity attracted tourists. Eddie Kidd enthused:

'Everybody wanted their picture taken next to the village sign. There's been a steady stream of visitors ever since, so we've gained some business.'

I'm delighted to hear it. There's just one thing. The sign needs updating. It should read 'Flash, the highest village in Britain at 1,558 feet.' Jump to it, lads!

IS THERE HONEY STILL FOR TEA?

Grantchester, Cambridgeshire

Grantchester will always be known as Rupert Brooke's village. One of Britain's best-loved poets spent many of his undergraduate and post-grad years seduced by its bucolic charm. The woods, the meadows and the river Cam absorbed him completely. He wrote to his girlfriend in 1909:

'I am in the country, in Arcadia; a rustic... I wander about barefoot and almost naked, surveying nature with a calm eye.'

The calm before the storm. Brooke was only 27 when he died during the war which followed. That was nearly a century ago, but if you close your eyes to a new housing estate on the horizon and ignore the cars wedged into every available space, Grantchester has barely changed in all that time. Its appeal is just as strong – a fact underlined by the throng of tourists when I dropped by.

Brooke would probably be astonished to know that scores of visitors filling the streets, the pubs and the cafes of this Domesday village were here for one reason only – him. Grantchester's other famous resident, Jeffrey Archer was seduced into buying the Old Vicarage because of its associations with Brooke. Business is booming at *The Orchard Tearooms* largely because of Brooke and people still come to swim in the river because *he* set the

trend. One of the public houses saw the writing on the wall – rather belatedly – and changed its name to *The Rupert Brooke* five years ago. I don't suppose they've ever looked back.

Brooke's pastoral dream came true when he left his rooms at Kings College, Cambridge because the town's hectic social life was distracting him. In fact, he was at the centre of it. His disappointing 2:2 degree in English was put down to a pleasure-seeking band of admirers who were in danger of derailing him, though Brooke too was partial to a little hedonism.

Grantchester, a mere two miles upstream from Cambridge, was the solution. Up to that point, the village had been the exclusive domain of Kings College's academic hierarchy. They actually owned most of the big houses and did a lot to preserve is character. Kings bought the Manor House in 1452 and used its grounds to supply the Fellows with pigeons and home-grown vegetables. It's still a farm today.

Grantchester had also become the morning-after rendezvous for revellers at Cambridge May Balls. Punting your girlfriend downstream for an *al fresco* breakfast was *de rigueur* for any aspiring lothario. The river was congested with hungover boaters in bow-ties steering tipsy partners in damp ball gowns and fancy hats through the dawn landscape with no guarantee of

Rupert Brooke's statue stands on Jeffrey Archer's driveway.

completing the journey. Champagne, Guinness and strawberries were the promise. I once did the trip from St. John's College and surprisingly lived to tell the tale. It's a challenging course. The riverbed gets extremely muddy and in several places, the water's too deep for the pole. Many a romantic voyage has ended in mid-stream humiliation. I was sad to hear that the Grantchester ritual has gone out of fashion.

It was a hot, sunny day when I went back to Grantchester Meadows for the first time in 40 years. Families were walking, picnicking or swimming in deep pools. A couple of canoeists paddled by, waving furiously. The bankside walk from Cambridge is known as the Grantchester Grind, which happens to be the title of a Tom Sharpe novel. Close by the river are the Orchard Tearooms where Brooke first lodged after leaving Kings.

A group of students persuaded the owner of the establishment, a Mrs Stevenson, to serve tea and scones in the orchard instead of on the front lawn. That was in 1897. The idea caught on. When I turned up, the orchard was heaving with people who sat on green deckchairs around small tables overhung with apple trees. A Vietnamese family in conical hats cut an especially attractive picture.

Illustrated notice boards attached to tree trunks inform guests that they're enjoying the same pleasures as Rupert Brooke, Virginia Woolf, E M Forster and Bertrand Russell the best part of a century ago. The Cambridge spies, Burgess, McClean, Philby and Blunt were also regular visitors. More recently, the Orchard Tearooms clientele included David Frost, John Cleese, Stephen Fry and Emma Thompson. The Orchard claims to have a more glittering guest list than any oasis in Britain.

Brooke's elitist friends, The Grantchester Group rechristened themselves the Neo-Pagans. They wallowed in sophisticated banter, wild parties, naked swimming sessions in the Cam and barefoot dances in Grantchester's dreamy woodlands. Brooke was in paradise, though arguably more distracted than ever. Before long, however, Mrs Stevenson tired of the Neo-Pagans and more or less gave them their marching orders. That was Rupert Brooke's cue to move into the Old Vicarage next door.

The Orchard Tearooms have attracted luminaries from Virginia Woolf to Prince Charles.

Granchester Mill Pond, with the early 18th century Mill House in the background.

He loved his new surroundings. Joy approached ecstasy. He wrote reams of poetry, ran every day to keep fit, swam at night and continued his efforts to win a fellowship at Kings. While on national service in Germany in 1912, he penned his most famous poem, 'The Old Vicarage.' It's a heavily romanticised eulogy of the building, of Grantchester itself and of England. The last two lines are as well known as anything from Shakespeare:

Stands the church clock at ten to three
And is there honey still for tea?

The 'Young Apollo' died of blood poisoning on a Greek island in the 1914-18 war. His heartbroken mother lost four sons in that conflict. Her reaction was to *buy* the Old Vicarage as a permanent tribute to them. The house has developed a personality of its own. So much so that a local historian, Christine Jennings, now in her 85th year, has written a hefty tome about it. Christine has become a close friend of Mary Archer and attended several of the theatrical events and summer parties for which the Old Vicarage is well known.

It's that time again!

Mary confesses she knew very little about Brooke until she came to live in his house and his village. Now she's written a book about him. Of course, it includes a photograph of the church clock – taken at 14.50 precisely! The Archers became so entranced by the legend of Rupert Brooke that they've installed a life-size statue of him in the drive of their famous home. It's said to be an inspiration for Jeffrey who writes his novels a few yards across the garden. As successful as Jeffrey is, he can't hope to attain the cult status of his predecessor. Nor will Mr Archer's lines have quite the same ring as these:

'I only know that you may lie
Day long and watch the Cambridge sky,
And, flower-lulled in sleepy grass
Hear the cool lapse of hours pass,
Until the centuries bend and blur
In Grantchester, in Grantchester.'

This archetypal Cotswold village was in ruins until a dynamic young businessman turned it into an industry.

THE BOTTOM LINE

Great Tew, Oxfordshire

With its thick cubes of honey-coloured ironstone and generous toppings of straw thatch you want to sink your teeth into, Great Tew delights all the senses. A bee drones; the creamy scent of hawthorn blossom fills the air; a child bounces a ball against a garden wall. It's so perfect, you think it can't be natural. And you're right. Great Tew isn't so much a village, more a business.

'For all the pretty postcards and chocolate box images, we're in trouble at the end of the year if it doesn't pay.'

So spoke Nick Johnston as he strolled along its heavily scented main street one clear summer's day. At the grand old age of 25, Nick became master of the Great Tew Estate – a hundred or so cottages and 4,000 acres of prime farmland. It sounds a dream job. It might be now but it wasn't then. After 50 years in public trusteeship, followed by a catastrophic spell under the ownership of Major Eustace Robb, Great Tew was a tip. The Cotswolds' shame. The deterioration seemed terminal. Sir Nikolaus Pevsner condemned it as:

'One of the most depressing in the country. Nothing has been done to prevent the decay of unused cottages, some of which are ruinous and will need to be entirely rebuilt.'

Eventually the estate fell into the hands of Matthew Boulton, the great West Midlands industrialist. He put his son in charge. Hopeless. In despair, the Boultons left it to a business partner who happened to be Nick Johnston's father. It looked and felt like a poisoned chalice. It needed the sort of drive and wisdom that successive owners/managers had been unable to provide. As luck would have it, Nick fancied the challenge even though the village shop and school were defunct. *The Falkland Arms* belonged to the brewery but it was still, indirectly, his concern.

There's been an extraordinary turnaround. The arable farming business is returning a handsome profit. They now have a modern and highly sophisticated grain store supplying farmers all over the UK. The quarry Nick reopened in 2000 is the only one in the country yielding superior grade ironstone for the house building industry. The dilapidated air strip is now a motor racing circuit attracting well-heeled customers who want to charge around in Ferraris and Aston Martins. And the annual Cornbury Music Festival – the biggest in the Cotswolds – is now staged in Great Tew. From negative equity, the village has become a market leader. It may even be a blueprint for rescuing moribund villages all over the country.

Says Nick:

'You've got to make the place work for its living. If you don't, there are no jobs to offer people and no money for refurbishing the next cottage.'

That might sound a little harsh, especially if you believe that villages are about communities and history, not balance sheets. The Lord of the Manor dismisses that idea as 'sentimental rubbish'. He says it's exactly why Great Tew almost perished. You would think that sentiment and business are impossible bedfellows, yet the reason Great Tew looks so edible and attracts visitors like a magnet, is precisely because Nick has paid so much attention to the bottom line. It's a commercially viable chocolate box.

Unsurprisingly, the estate has trodden on a few toes. One old woman complained that she was driven out of the village. She and her family had rented one of the farms for generations but couldn't afford to buy when Nick put it on the market. His reaction:

'It is sad but we can no longer guarantee a job for life for anyone. It has to be a question of balance, otherwise the whole thing will shut down.'

Great Tew may still look like a sleepy farming village, but don't be fooled. Twenty farms have been whittled down to three. Sixty per cent of the villagers are tenants but Nick has opened it up to 'outsiders' who don't mind paying commercial rents. As you'd expect, the fees are high, but the living's good. Those who work on the estate have their cottages maintained with the proceeds. There's money in the kitty for a rainy day. For every person who complains that Great Tew isn't what it was, there are two who say 'thank goodness'.

KICKING THE BOTTLE

Hallaton, Leicestershire

It was the coldest Easter on record when I eventually witnessed one of the world's most testosterone-fuelled rituals. The Hare Pie Scramble and Bottle Kicking between Hallaton and Medbourne didn't disappoint. It was so cold I thought about taking part just to keep warm. The thought didn't last long.

We're not sure how many centuries have slipped under Hallaton's makeshift bridge since war was declared. A visit to its charming tin museum failed to enlighten me on that point. Talking of tin, rumour says the contest dates from the Iron Age but you know what rumour's like.

Snow decorated the hilltops like sugar on a mince pie. The wind arrived in knife thrusts from Scandinavia. Still they came to marvel at this gruesome display of inter-village machismo. One of the rules is that there aren't any. You don't have to live in Hallaton or Medbourne to qualify. No bottles are involved in the contest – and they don't do much kicking. The 'ball' is a wooden beer keg guaranteed to break your toes if you're daft enough to attempt a David Beckham.

Strolling uphill to the *Fox Inn*, I bumped into Sandra Marlow, a former resident, who proudly announced that she'd been coming to the Bottle Kicking for 50 years. She needed to stay in more! Sandra told me that her husband and four sons had taken part at different times during the half century, so she had to lend moral support. The only hiatus was in 2001 when Foot and Mouth rendered the event null and void.

The Fox was already bulging. Bee Gees music blared from a stall in the car park; smoke rose from the ubiquitous hot dog stand. I felt sorry for the Scottish Pipe Band shivering alongside their instruments. This was no time for kilts. None of them came from Scotland either.

After a glass of the local brew, Bottle Kicking cider, I transferred to the *Bewicke Arms*, where most of the ceremonials would take place. Hundreds huddled around the Butter Cross for warmth. They included a photographer from the Market Harborough Mail whose 23rd successive tour of duty this was. The most memorable

of those was when Robbie Coltrane lent his bulk to the proceedings during the filming of the television series, 'B-road Britain.'

'Nice chap,' said the photographer, 'but he spent most of his time sitting in the car.'

He was no fool then. The distant swirl of bagpipes sent a different shiver through us. It meant the procession was heading our way. The standard bearer in mediaeval dress carried a pole with the carving of a brass hare on top. A brass monkey might have been more appropriate! Then I saw the star of the show. Her name was Lynne Allan and she's been carrying her home-baked hare pie in the vanguard of the procession for the last ten years. Contrary to popular myth, it *is* a genuine hare pie. Lynne's husband, Phil was insulted that anyone should think otherwise:

'People who claim it's minced beef are talking rubbish. We collected two whole hares from a game butcher in Uppingham and cooked them in red wine. I should know – the house stank of hare!'

The pie was blessed by the vicar on the church steps, then broken up and tossed to 'the poor'. Those of us suffering in the double dip recession were extremely grateful. I tasted a sliver out of the baking tray before it was flung to the multitude. Delicious. A shame to throw it away like that!

By now, the crowd had swollen to 2,000 or more. Blue faces creased with cold; gloved hands clutching at thin air for a crumb of pie. I tried to imagine the beginnings of this glorious nonsense. The story goes that two women from Hallaton were stopped in their tracks by a bull while crossing Hare Pie Hill one day in the distant past.

A gory ending was avoided when a hare sprinted past, spooking the bull. As a show of relief and gratitude, the women baked

Left: For one day each year, Hallaton throws caution to the wind and unleashes centuries of frustration on its neighbouring village.

Right: It'll end in tears, chaps.

a hare pie (not *that* hare, I hope), entertained the village, and decreed that food and drink would be offered to the peasants each Easter Monday from then onwards. The neighbouring village of Medbourne went and spoiled the celebrations by launching a dawn raid and running off with all the beer. Hallaton has never forgiven them.

Back in the present, we legged it across Hallaton brook to Hare Pie Hill where hypothermia seemed unavoidable. At ten minutes past three, someone launched a cask into the air and a hundred warriors in varying stages of inebriation threw themselves after it. The accompanying battle cry could be heard in Market Harborough.

Following the play was tricky. The cask only appeared momentarily. Then, out of nowhere, an optimistic youth seized it and attempted a solo dash for the brook. Poor fool was virtually disembowelled before he'd gone

Leaping towards the brook - a contestant breaks free from the pack clutching the cask. He'll soon regret it.

five yards! The scrum crashed its way through hedges and fences as though they weren't there.

Three quad bikes converted into ambulances patrolled the hillside to scoop up the inevitable casualties.

The game can last until midnight. To score a 'goal' Medbourne have to touch down in *their* brook, three-quarters of a mile away. Likewise, Hallaton try to deposit the cask in theirs. Best of three casks wins.

As daylight slipped away, so did the spectators. I walked back through the

Before the contest: all mouth and trousers

gathering gloom accompanied by one of the marshalls, an ex-paratrooper. Gazing back at the steaming mass of humanity on the hillside, he said:

'You must think we're mad to do this, but it's a fantastic event. I once came all the way back from the Falklands to take part. I had 48 hours leave. Flew in, played in the winning team and flew back.'

I asked if he was serious. He was. He said it was a pleasure to get back to Port Stanley for some peace and quiet.

As usual, the winners on this occasion were Hallaton and as usual, Medbourne were outnumbered. The score was 2-1, which was poetic justice. If Medbourne hadn't hijacked Hallaton's celebrations all those centuries ago, they'd have been left alone.

Now then, what do they do for the rest of the year around here?

PLANES, WHAT PLANES?

Harmondsworth and Sipson, Middlesex

Like a giant albatross, the Emirates jet heaves itself above St. Mary's church before screaming off to Rio or Delhi or Kuala Lumpur. No-one in Harmondsworth gives it a glance. In neighbouring Sipson, there's barely anyone who can!

These two communities are modern plague villages. The plague is Heathrow and its third runway. The prognosis isn't good. Sipson's heart has already been torn out. Most long-term residents have taken the BAA shilling and cleared off. Businesses have closed down. All that's left is a butcher, Gerald Storr, who talks of 'tangible desolation', a hairdresser who's lost the bulk of her customers, and a Bangladeshi restaurant which just hangs in there, as Bangladeshi restaurants have a knack of doing.

Oh yes, and a school called Heathrow Primary, standing on the site of the original parish of Heathrow, long since devastated. Many Sipson homes, bought by BAA at market value plus ten per cent (with removal fees thrown in), look sad and neglected. Nettles strangle the roses. The message is loud and clear:

Above: As the jets roar over Harmondsworth, village life goes on regardless.

104

'We'd had enough of protesting. Nobody listened anyway. We took the money and ran.'

Harmondsworth is a different story. Although two decades of demonstrating against the third runway have inevitably taken their toll, this village refuses to buckle. The green's planted with hyacinths and salvias; mothers meet their gleeful toddlers from school and buy sweets in the general store; the one remaining farmer tends his shire horses within 500 yards of the runway and watches dispassionately as another albatross soars into the sky from an apparently standing start.

Meanwhile, in the lounge of the splendid Harmondsworth House, Nancy's enjoying a farewell coffee before jetting back to New Orleans. The seventeenth century bed and breakfast establishment in Summerhouse Lane couldn't be handier for the airport. 'Give me this instead of the Marriott any day,' Nancy enthuses.

So why the contrast between neighbouring villages which watched with equal foreboding as a small military aerodrome ballooned into one of the world's busiest commercial hubs?

The obvious difference is that British Airports Authority failed to offer financial inducements to Harmondsworth, on the grounds that the elusive runway would leave most of their village intact. Sipson, in contrast, *was* the runway. If this arrangement left any rancour in Harmondsworth, I'm not sure. Whether there'd be a similar rush to the exit, I doubt. Harmondsworth is less suburban – and, crazy though it sounds for a community enclosed by the M4, the airport and their attendant infrastructure – more of a village?

There's a delightful stream running through a small area of parkland; nearby anglers catch carp as Jumbos thunder overhead every 45 seconds; the *Five Bells* is a warm, friendly tavern; the church is active in the community and, most notably, Britain's finest and biggest tithe barn occupies half a meadow just behind it. The Great Barn, now cared for by English Heritage after a period of decay, is 192 feet long, 38 feet wide and 37 feet tall. It's open to visitors twice a month.

But of course, Harmondsworth isn't everyone's cup of tea. Aeroplanes make a continuous drone rather than a deafening roar. Then there's air pollution. An older villager complained about fuel from the heavens rendering his vegetable crop inedible. And the traffic is heavy. To cap it all, the prospect of a third runway still hangs over them. How much longer can the uncertainty go on? There's even a local rumour that not one but *two* new runways are on the horizon – one for European destinations, the other intercontinental.

Whether that's true or false, poor old Harmondsworth seems to be permanently on tenterhooks. It's a blighted village. Residents have little hope of selling their homes even if they wanted to. Through it all, they soldier on, hoping that BAA will put its third runway somewhere else. Whatever strategy prevails, it's too late for Sipson.

Jackfield was once a bustling river port full of pubs and brothels where beer-swilling trowmen hauled their boats up and down the Ironbridge Gorge.

THE VILLAGE WHICH BROKE IN HALF

Jackfield, Shropshire

Until you get there, Jackfield's just a possibility. Neither the AA nor the RAC have it listed in their road atlases nor marked on the map. It could be a subtle device to deter unwanted visitors. It made my journey a lottery. I pointed my car in the general direction of Ironbridge and hoped.

It worked. Jackfield definitely exists although not in its entirety. What's left of the original port holds on tightly to both banks of the river Severn. Bent, cracked and buckled it may be, but erased it certainly isn't. As I write, the local authority is grappling with subsidence problems, a full 61 years after a catastrophe which threatened to wipe it off the map. Jackfield's history on-going.

Back in the 1800s when smoke belched from its chimneys and the air was as thick as gravy, they called it the 'fag end of the universe'. Jackfield was a product of the industrial revolution. A maelstrom of a river port with different cargoes being loaded or unloaded all day long. Every adult was employed. Work was tough but pleasure was available at the drop of an anchor. Sailors thought it was a perk of the job.

Smoke, grime, booze and crime was a volatile mix. At the hub was Jackfield Encaustic and Decorative Tile Works where 700 men fired the clay which turned this once-lovely riverbank into the heart of Britain's tile making industry. They've found other uses for the factory but it's intact and still bears the famous name in bold lettering along its flank.

In those wild, raucous days, beer-swilling trowmen hauled their flat-bottomed boats up and down the Ironbridge Gorge. They carried grain as well as coal, wood and tiles. The port was heaving with bars and whorehouses. Sailors who never saw the sea sampled everything else a seaport could offer. At its height – or depth – Jackfield boasted no fewer than thirty brothels. Some of them are still there, converted into pubs and houses.

But the good times couldn't last forever. Nature, provoked and plundered by industrialists for 150 years, eventually hit back. Clay mine owners repeatedly neglected to pump water out of the shafts, creating a time bomb. Sure enough, in April 1952, Jackfield broke in half and slid into the Severn. Roads disappeared.

The railway line, a major umbilical cord, lay twisted in knots like a length of wire. It still does. Jackfield's industrial revolution was over in 24 hours. A former resident who'd moved to London recalled his horror on seeing a News Chronicle placard in Piccadilly: 'Village sinks into river.' It was national and international news.

I'm delighted to report that Jackfield has not only survived but prospers in relative anonymity. That is, until the brass band festival comes to town each summer. Musicians from Shropshire and neighbouring counties entertain dining guests in the courtyard of the old tile works. It's delightful.

The population has clearly shrunk and they don't make tiles any more. However, the village is rather proud of its ornate Victorian church made entirely of local bricks and tiles. A short distance away are the remains of Mrs Dirk's old tin sweetshop, noted for home-made humbugs. You'll have to imagine the line of school kids outside.

Now that we've learned to live with potholes, driving through Jackfield ceases to hold the same terrors. Nevertheless, the main artery is the track of the old Severn Valley Railway, so be warned. It's not so much a road as a collection of ruts and ridges. The ancient high street comes to a premature end after 150 yards. A couple of metal rails, themselves broken and twisted, mark the point at which the asphalt plunges into what has become a woodland path.

The terraced houses, along with the remainder of the road, have gone. All that remains of the early settlement is the *Half Moon* pub (wouldn't you just know?). Unlike the houses that pressed against it, the inn was built on solid rock, instead of sand. They had their priorities right! Across the river stands another lone edifice, half concealed by vegetation. This is the old Lloyds School, the remnant of an adjoining hamlet of the same name. The parish of Lloyds slid into the water too.

Strolling around this ghost town of a thousand cracks, where splintered rooftops peep through the foliage, you become aware that nature's reclamation has turned a beast into a beauty. Jackfield has become a desirable place to live. If you want a holiday cottage, join the queue. One of the brothels is now a delightful bed and breakfast establishment called the Severn Trow, run by a couple from neighbouring Ironbridge. They were quick to pounce when the property came onto the market in 2008. The history of Jackfield has become an all-consuming hobby for them, as indeed it was for the previous owner, Pauline Hannigan. Initially she was coy about its shady background, but decided to make a virtue of it – if you'll forgive the expression. She restored the brothel cubicle and turned it into a washroom. The hole in the wall through which Madam spied on her employees and customers, stays in place.

The Severn Trow was as dilapidated as its morals when Pauline arrived. The roof caved in 25 years earlier, hiding a rare treasure even by Jackfield's standards. When she and her husband cleared the debris, they discovered a stunning mosaic floor made of traditional one-inch square tiles coloured red, blue, black and white. The belief is that they'd been smuggled out of the factory little by little and assembled illegally. 'One piece at a time,' as Johnny Cash would sing. The mosaic is worth a small fortune.

That's Jackfield for you. Abraham Darby's famous iron bridge at one end of the valley, an unsightly coal-fired power station at the other and, almost lost in the middle, the village that cartographers forgot. I'd politely suggest the motoring organisations include it in their next editions. If you fancy a trip to Jackfield – and I recommend it – go sooner rather than later. It's still slipping.

Jackfield paid dearly in 1952 for the failure to pump water out of its disused shafts ... and it's still paying.

EARTH QUAKERS

Jordans, Buckinghamshire

Modern life tends to pass this Quaker village by. Although Jordans sits smack in the middle of Buckingham-shire commuter belt, it has little in common with the upmarket Beaconsfield and Chalfont St. Giles which preen themselves on its doorstep. Curiously perhaps, it falls under the local government control of Chalfont Parish Council.

I was struck by the lack of sporting facilities. Nobody *plays* Jordans at anything – least of all darts because it doesn't possess a pub. Alcohol is taboo. Cricket flourished for years but became a *cause célèbre* in 1994 when the village club successfully defended an injunction to get the game banned. The plaintiff resented cricket balls flying into his garden and threatening his windows. This magnificent slice of trivia received international coverage because it encapsulated everything about the English psyche. Even Panama television went big on it! Unfortunately the cricket club closed soon afterwards through lack of interest.

Jordans is not a place you'd bust a gut to visit. It's functional, some would say basic. That doesn't present a problem to the people who live there. I think they're happy to be out of the swim. There is, of course, more to it than that – notably a togetherness which would delight its Quaker founders. That, after all, is the village *raison d'être*.

However, my introduction to this offbeat community was discouraging. I arrived to find a village of uniform houses and uniform people who drank tea and didn't smile much. I repaired to the Friends Meeting House, an impressive, if rather austere building in its own grounds where Quakers have gathered since it was built in 1688. It's one of the oldest meeting houses in the country. William Penn, the founder of Pennsylvania, is one of several Quaker pioneers buried in the grounds.

Presently, a woman in a large, flowery sunhat agreed – it took some persuading – to be interviewed for our television programme about the essence of Quakerism. Was it a religion or an attitude? What were the overriding principles? Where did the name come from? Her replies were stand-offish. They convinced me that The Society of Friends needed Saatchi and Saatchi. I was wrong. PR is the last thing they want. Quakers don't seek attention. The sunhat was out of character.

The Green at Jordans and The Friends' Meeting House which was destroyed by fire in 2005 and had to be rebuilt.

Several years on, I can report that Jordans is more or less unaltered. Unspectacular red brick houses stand to attention around the village green as they have for 125 years. The only change, thankfully, is the attitude. It has softened considerably. My return visit began with a déjà vu moment. Nigel Morgan, a pillar of Jordans' society was reading his newspaper at a table on the green, precisely as he was the last time I called. Only the headlines were different. Nigel was born and brought up here. He's intensely proud of his village. In cool spring sunshine, it looked neat, if rather soulless. Children played on the swings. There was an encouraging stream of people to and from the village shop.

'Greetings!' called Nigel as if I'd never been away. 'I enjoyed your TV programme.'

Not only did he remember it, he could recite chunks of it verbatim! This man was not to be trifled with! Nigel returned to Jordans after emigrating to Vancouver. 'Vancouver was fine but I missed home. Had it been Birmingham I'd have stayed out there!'

His waspish sense of humour was somewhat out of place in such a serious place. That's because, notwithstanding his devotion to Jordans, Nigel *isn't* a Quaker. Nor was it a requirement when the village was conceived in 1922 by the Society of Friends and other conscientious objectors to war. The idea was to create a self-owning and self-supporting community where artisans could ply their craft in a free and friendly atmosphere. Although Quakers make up only 20% of the Jordans' population today, their philosophy holds firm. As one of the elders, Ann Floyd explained:

'It's an awareness that everybody matters. We go out of our way to help and encourage people from all backgrounds.'

Many of the houses belonging to Jordans Village Ltd. have been sold but the company still collects rent from 61 properties, including four old peoples' houses which were built in the last few years. The shop's run separately by Jordans Village Store Ltd. It's bright, well-stocked with hams and cheeses, and lovingly tended by a rota of volunteers. However, I caught sight of the minutes of the 2011 AGM, pinned to the notice board. They didn't make pleasant reading. The shop had a £9,600 deficit. 'This cannot go on,' the AGM was told. A whip-round postponed the crisis but it won't go away. Younger residents are attracted by supermarkets; the old faithfuls die out. It's a familiar tale. The shop manager, Jane Spoerry said everything would be fine if all its customers spent an additional £6 a week. It's a big 'if'.

It was time to revisit the famous Friends Meeting House, built immediately after the Declaration of Indulgence made it possible for religious groups to congregate indoors. Before 1688, Quakers were persecuted. Meetings were broken up by local justices and attendees marched off to prison. It hasn't exactly been plain sailing since. The Meeting House was practically destroyed by fire in 2005. Fortunately the inner sanctum remained intact. With its wooden benches; separate sections for male and female attenders, and above eye-height windows to prevent distraction, there's a slight feeling of incarceration. Odd that. Quakerism is open-minded and free-thinking by definition.

At least Nigel Morgan can see the lighter side of life. He told me the subject of a public house for Jordans cropped up from time to time. On the last occasion, he suggested a suitable name for it might be *The Jolly Quaker*. A voice from the back growled: 'Is there such a thing?'

William Penn, founder of Pennysylvania, was buried in the village. Below right: the Jordans community shop.

PLOUGHMAN'S LUNCH

Laxton, Nottinghamshire

In a part of Nottinghamshire where Robin Hood robbed the rich to feed the poor, a village called Laxton upholds his egalitarian principles. This is where the small farmer is King. He works for the Queen. His right to till the soil is carved in tablets of stone. It makes Laxton unique. Students from all over the world come to marvel at the only remaining example of an agricultural system rooted in peasantry.

In stark contrast to the monoculture which has turned England's pastures into arable factories, farming families in Laxton labour side by side on narrow strips of land – some barely wide enough to take a combine. You could call it collectivism, except that once the farmers have paid their peppercorn rent to the Crown and observed the strict rules of crop rotation, they're free to make whatever profit they can.

Above: I've never come across a more closely-bonded agricultural community than this. But can it last?

Farmers are given a token fine if they stray into each other's strips.

Laxton is England's only remaining open fields village. If that sounds totalitarian, let me assure you that the outcome is truly uplifting. Here we have a fully focussed, thoroughly bonded community where a healthy percentage of the population earns a living from the land. How old-fashioned is that? Peter Brown, landlord of *The Dovecote Inn*, was unaware of Laxton's history but sensed it was a special place when he drove down from Bolton, looking for a pub to run. It was a rainy winter's day and the old mining area around Ollerton wasn't appealing. He wanted to turn back but his wife persuaded him to drive on.

'The landscape suddenly opened up,' he said. 'The village looked great. The pub immediately felt right.'

Laxton's that sort of place. It may be a heritage site but it's also a living entity. I haven't come across any other community where so many residents work in the village and celebrate the agricultural calendar with such gusto. They fill the church on Lammas Day when farmers traditionally give thanks for the first ear of corn, and they beat the bounds on Rogation Sunday – a date that passes most parishes by. Harvest Festivals are like they used to be. The cripplingly wet summer of 2012 brought tears; the consolation in 2013 inspired a carnival atmosphere.

Yet there's an air of uncertainty about Laxton. The open fields system, though fair and honourable and drenched in nostalgia, struggles to make economic sense. The older farmers know they're dinosaurs. Everyone's aware that this way of life can't be artificially sustained *ad infinitum*.

Open fields date back to William the Conqueror. The system was eventually broken up by Enclosures Act. Manorial estates were fenced off in the 1800 and 1900s and ordinary folk were denied their right to grow crops and graze animals. Farming changed forever. But not in Laxton. Because of an unusual set of circumstances, the village escaped the full force of the Enclosures Act. For one thing, its farmers couldn't agree on the best way of enclosing the land; for another, the major landowner, Earl Manvers, had blown his money on Thoresby Hall and couldn't afford it. At different periods since then, Parliament has given Laxton its blessing to continue with its open fields.

I stepped into this time-warp on the last Thursday of November as a guest of Stuart Rose, a farmer and clerk to an ancient institution called Gaits and Commoners. The date is significant. It's when a team of jurors, chosen from the farmers *by* the farmers, makes an annual inspection of the fields. If a colleague has overstepped the mark and strayed into a neighbouring strip – or left the dykes and adjoining flower meadows (called sykes) untidy, he faces the wrath of the jurors at the official Court Leet the following Thursday. If prosecuted, he'll be ordered to pay a fine. He is, of course, entitled to plead his innocence but the chances are he'll be ten quid lighter when he leaves. Jurors aren't renowned for their leniency.

In case you think I'm in fairyland, you're right. This relic of manorial government, surviving from the Middle Ages, helps to make Laxton what it is. The Court Leet enjoys a unique legal status. It's presided over by a solicitor. Fairyland with teeth!

Apart from Southwell Minster and Sherwood Forest, Nottinghamshire is an unspectacular county – and Sherwood Forest is only a forest if you use your imagination. So I was pleasantly surprised by the rolling landscape around Laxton – a forgotten part of the county. Laxton itself was more attractive than I remembered. Red pantile roofs look good on red bricks houses. Very Nottinghamshire.

Its most unusual feature is that all the farms and farm buildings are in the village, as opposed to out in the country. In fact many are in the high street. This is a direct consequence of open fields agriculture. Because the land was divided into relatively small strips, there was no room for buildings. It's better this way. The streets are full of tractors – mainly of the vintage variety – and the village is full of life. Stuart announced proudly:

'We have twenty farming families in Laxton. There's always help at hand. The next village, Kneesall, is owned and managed as one farm. There isn't a single member of the population involved in agriculture. That tells a story.'

Although Stuart was effectively in charge of proceedings on Inspection Day, the trailerful of farmers heading for the fields on an overcast Thursday knew the routine by heart. Sitting on hay bales and bumping over rutted tracks, we began to chew the cud, as they say. One of the jurors, David Sayer turned to me:

'You must think this is Mickey Mouse farming. We've only got a hundred acres each.'

Like the other jurors, David was born and has spent his life in Laxton. The average age of the group was 67. That tells another story. Dear old Colin Cree would be 84 next birthday. He had doubts about the future:

'A hundred acres isn't much more than a garden. What young farmer will be interested in that? The system only provides us with a living because of subsidies.'

David Sayer seconded that, adding:

'We're proud of the open fields but they're a nightmare to farm. They're a mile away from our machinery.'

The oldest passenger in the trailer had been quiet until now. Bill Haigh from Manor Farm has seen 53 harvests since he began farming at Laxton. He's 87 now and more hopeful than some of his colleagues:

'The system should carry on. Surely someone will follow us?'

Bill's optimism impressed me. We spent the next two hours tramping the muddy edges of the arable strips and hammering in stakes to re-mark the boundaries. Despite his years, Bill put in a shift. The wind blew; the crows flew; the jurors talked shop. The mood was more serious than I expected – this wasn't a 'jolly'. In the distance, a dramatic plume of water vapour from British Sugar's Newark plant mushroomed high into the sky as though simulating Mururoa Atoll. Sugarbeet is the main crop on that side of Nottinghamshire. Winter is harvest time and hectic. Laxton, in contrast, was becalmed. Wheat, barley and rape had long since been gathered in.

The banter continued as the inspection neared its end:

'This is good soil for making bricks!'

'My brother baled someone else's strip by mistake.'

'All we need is a shower o' rain one day and a shower o' muck the next.'

The tractor deposited us back at *The Dovecote* where the jurors feasted on their time-honoured lunch of roast beef and Yorkshire pudding. It was followed by a meeting to draw up the list of transgressors. Their cases would come before the court in a week's time. I wasn't allowed into the meeting. I took the opportunity to nip across the pub car park to the all-day visitor centre. It explains Laxton's complicated story and includes the copy of an ancient map kept at the Bodleian Library in Oxford. The level of detail is remarkable. It's reckoned to be one of the most important maps in the country.

Stuart joined me in the bar when the meeting was over. At 57 he's one of the youngest farmers in the village and is immersed in its tradition. How much, I wondered, had the open fields system contributed to Laxton's identity? He replied:

'I only have to click my fingers and we can organise a fundraising event in moments. Without asking I'd know who's making the trifle and who's running the barbecue. That's how united we are. We're not *all* farmers, by the way. There are other professionals and retired people too. I could make a better living somewhere else but that's not the point. I *want* to live here. My tap root goes down a long way. If you dropped me in any of the fields in the dead of night, I'd know exactly where I was. I know all the trees. I've climbed most of them!'

Between them, Stuart and his colleagues farm 1,400 acres and pay around £60 an acre for the privilege. The land passed from Earl Manver to the Ministry of Agriculture in 1952. The Ministry sold it to the Crown Estate Commissioners in 1981. The Crown gave a parliamentary undertaking to protect the open field system *sine die*. The Crown also own houses in Laxton. According to the tenants, the current landlord is 'bottom-line conscious'. In other words, everything has to make a profit.

That's why two young women from Carter Jonas, the land agent acting on behalf of the Crown Estate, accompanied us on the field inspection. It was their duty to provide a feasibility study for Laxton's future.

One of the farmers told me he'd considered buying the land from the Crown Commissioners himself. Apparently they 'didn't want to sell to someone who would die.' Presumably they'd prefer a private equity fund. That message seemed to imply that they'd listen to offers – a point I raised with the Crown's East Midlands portfolio manager, Robin Clarke. Here's his answer:

'Our remit in 1981 was to keep it going on the understanding that we'd maintain the system.'

Yes, I know that. But the farmers say it's not financially viable.

'It's still working and we're keeping to our remit. There has to be a return.'

Have you considered selling?

'No.'

The Crown Estate Commissioners own the land around Laxton.

Umm. Well, the Court Leet duly sat on the first Thursday in December. It was a quaint and colourful event. The first task was to fine the twelve absentees 2p each for their non-appearance. That'll teach 'em! Then came the case of farmer Nick Gent, whose ploughing had left a quantity of soil on a roadway between the strips. Tut, tut. He apologised, paid his £10 and left without a stain on his character. The surprise – to me anyway – was a rap on the knuckles for Stuart Rose himself. The esteemed clerk had been careless while spraying his crop. Some of the insecticide had drifted onto a syke (SSSI grassland). He won't do that again. Afterwards, a new set of jurors was sworn in for 2014 and business was concluded for another year.

How long will these ancient rituals last, I asked the man with the portfolio.

'I'm optimistic that the Laxton system will carry on, ' said Mr. Clarke.

But where's the next batch of farmers coming from?

'Some new ones have joined already. I'm sure there'll be more.'

Bill Haigh, Colin Cree *et al* – you can stand easy.

WHOLLY ISLAND

Lindisfarne, Northumberland

From whichever angle you approach it, Lindisfarne is visually stimulating, spiritually uplifting and historically fascinating. One of the Wonders of Britain. If you travel the east coast line from Kings Cross to Berwick on Tweed, the view across Northumberland's magnolia beaches to an island with a castle on top, is worth the ticket alone.

Through the train window, Holy Island can fool you into thinking it's deserted. Get closer and you discover a living, breathing community with families who go back generations. Families who organise their lives around the tides which cast them adrift for several hours a day. Families who are conditioned to extreme weather and rough seas.

There's a sense of adventure each time you drive, cycle or walk across the causeway that connects Lindisfarne to the rest of Northumberland. Some of the route will be puddled from the previous tide. It reminds you that the clock is ticking. Unless you are staying on the island, you may have to retrace your steps sooner than planned. The sea, of course, sets its own agenda. For example, at the end of August, there's a nine-hour window for crossing, from late morning to mid-evening. By September, the window shrinks to the size of a porthole. There's no such thing as a nine-to-five job for workers travelling from the mainland. They can only report for duty when the moon permits.

Just as it did in the ancient past, nature's drawbridge gives the resident population of Holy Island Village protection from invading hordes. Then it was Vikings; this time it's tourists. Once the waters recede, holidaymakers swarm across. The hardier ones do it barefoot on mud and sand, following The Pilgrims' Way. Those who depend on the influx – publicans, shopkeepers, and bed and breakfast hosts – raise a cheer. Likewise the purveyors of Lindisfarne Mead, a fortified wine produced exclusively on the island. Two glasses of that and you'd swear there were longboats on the horizon.

Left: Lindisfarne organises its life around the tides. Villagers are cut off for several hours a day.

Not until you leave the gift shops, the winery, the museum and cottages behind you and take the long walk to the castle, does Holy Island's isolation hit you. Fishing boats wait for the tide to activate them. The wind blows hard even on a good day. Clouds are usually gathering somewhere. Painters are attracted here by the ever-changing light and scale of this landscape-cum-seascape. On the shore, your eye is drawn by three upturned fishing boats converted into storage sheds. Simple but extremely photogenic.

The sixteenth century castle is pure Disney. It sits on a conical volcanic mound. You can hardly see the join. It's as though castle and mound had been turned on a potter's wheel. The building began life as a fortification against the marauding Scots, only to be redesigned as an Edwardian home by Sir Edwin Lutyens 250-odd years later. Nobody lives here now. The last baron, Sir Edward de Stein, ran out of money and left it to the National Trust in 1960. Nick Lewis has the enviable task of running it. He told me:

'I'm lucky to work in such an iconic location. Lindisfarne Castle may not be in the same bracket as Blenheim Palace but it's a vital landmark for the northeast.'

Although the tides can play havoc with timetables, Nick and his staff handle around 70,000 visitors a year and manage a couple of dozen weddings too. It was close to this spot that Saint Aidan docked in 635 AD, having sailed from Iona. By invitation of the King of Northumbria, he built a monastery. Come the dissolution of the monasteries, most of the masonry was used on the castle.

Another monk, Saint Cedd, made an equally risky voyage to spread Christianity south. He left Holy Island and reached the Dengie peninsula in Essex where he erected a wooden chapel and continued his evangelism. Refashioned in stone, the chapel is now recognized by many as the smallest cathedral in the UK.

But back to Holy Island and its current evangelist, Rev. Dr. Paul Collins. He first visited Lindisfarne while reading theology at Durham University. It made a lasting impression. Eventually, after a spell at Bognor Regis on the Sussex coast, Reverend Collins saw an advert for a vacancy on Holy Island and seized his chance. Vicar of Holy Island – it doesn't get much better.

As you might expect, Holy Islanders are mightily attached to their piece of rock. Few more so than Tommy Douglas who recently retired after half a century on the high seas. Tommy began fishing for crab and lobster as soon as he left school in the 1950s. It was a natural progression. There were nine fishing boats in those days, some of them part-owned by two or maybe three fishermen. Now the number is down to six boats and fourteen fishermen. But, as Tommy said:

'There's still a good enough living to be made. Lobsters fetch a decent price in Spain, Italy and Portugal.

The view of Lindisfarne Castle from trains on the east-coast line to Berwick is worth the price of the ticket alone.

Personally speaking though, I'm glad of a rest now. It means I can enjoy the island. I couldn't live anywhere else in the world but here.'

That view is endorsed by Sue Massey, a Yorkshire lass who owns the Oasis Café. It's a little less demanding than the Lindisfarne Hotel, which she and her husband bought almost on a whim after a holiday in Northumberland. That was 42 happy years ago, but they needed a break. Café trade is steady in the summer, becalmed in winter. Sue shuts the Oasis after bonfire night and, apart from the occasional weekend, doesn't open again until February half term.

The months in between are bracing to say the least. From my experience though, there are a few more invigorating exercises than a mid-winter walk along those broad, windswept beaches on the other side of the water. I watched a fishing boat return to shore and thought of St. Cedd, battling through those rough seas alone, nearly 1,400 years ago. He was determined to spread the gospel and the only way was Essex!

WHAT'S IN A NAME?

Llanfairpwllgwyngyllgogerychwyrndrobwllllantysiliogogogoch, Anglesey

According to the online ticket agency I use for rail journeys, Llanfairpwllgwyngyllgogerychwyrndrobwll-lantysiliogogogoch railway station didn't exist. Um. In that case, how come thousands of people have their photographs taken there? The station is world famous. Trainline kept repeating that there was no such place. The closest I could get was Bangor.

I phoned Arriva Trains Wales to double check. A foreign voice answered. I was through to a call centre in India. Oh dear. Even if I pronounced it properly, I had a negligible chance of explaining to a resident of Himachal Pradesh that I wanted to get to Llanfairpwllgwyngyllgogerychwyrndrobwllllantysiliogogogoch – and expecting him to understand.

I eventually discovered that the station *was* listed on the rail network but abbreviated to Llanfairpwll for obvious reasons. It was, apparently, a request stop. That means if you forgot to tell the guard that you wanted to alight, you'd be in Holyhead before you could say Cymry am byth (Long live Wales!). Guard? I couldn't even *find* one in an overcrowded train heading for the holiday playgrounds of Prestatyn, Colwyn Bay and Llandudno. I'd have to sneak into the driver's cab and whisper; 'Would you mind dropping me off at St. Mary's Church in a hollow of white hazel near the swirling whirlpool of the church of St Tysilio, please?' in his unsuspecting ear. That's the translation by the way.

We reached Bangor. Mine was the next stop – the first station on Anglesey, or Ynys Môn if you prefer. Fortunately, the guard surfaced in the nick of time, reeled off the names of a clutch of stations in Anglesey and asked if there were any takers. When I reached my unpronounceable destination, parents on the far platform were ordering their reluctant offspring to cross the footbridge and stand under the sign for a photograph. Prefer-ably with hands *out* of pockets. It's a routine repeated approximately 100,000 times a year. Not exactly the Taj Mahal but a priceless addition to the family album.

LLANFAIRPWLLGWYNGYLLGOGERYCHWYRNDROBWLLLLANTYSILIOGOGOGOCH

Llan-vire-pooll-guin-gill-go-ger-u-queern-drob-ooll-llandus-ilio-gogo-goch

ARRIVA   Arriva Trains Wales / Trenau Arriva Cymru

Way Out ←

Holyhead →

Above: Say no more!

This is a major tourist spot. The unidentified tailor whose idea it was to give this village the longest name in Britain and the third longest in the world, deserves a posthumous gong. It was a brilliant publicity stunt. Historically known as Llanfairpwllgwyngyll, this little community agreed to have its name stretched in 1860 to maximise its new role as a railway stop. The Britannia Bridge had enabled the Euston line to be extended across the Menai Straits to Holyhead. Some historians reckon it was the brainchild of a cobbler from Menai Bridge, but I'll stick with the tailor. More than 150 years later, visitors still come in their droves to photograph the name. I doubt he could have foreseen that.

Although the station itself is little used, the car park is full. I watched coaches from Llandudno and Caernarvon discharge their passengers directly into the giant James Pringle Weavers' shopping mall as though it was statutory. They queued to have their passports stamped with the 58-letter name and to buy everything from chocolates to blankets to washing machines. Then it was the short walk to the platform for photographs. James Pringle Weavers paid for the restoration of the station building which, although closed for business, at least gives tourists a backdrop for their pictures. They need wide-angle lenses for Llanfairpwllgwyngyllgogerychwyrndrobwllllantysiliogogogoch.

But they miss the best bit. Instead of retail therapy, they should take a walk down to the waterfront. Having been persuaded by Peter Davies, the tourist office supervisor, to look a little deeper into Llanfairpwll life, I discovered several interesting things. This village which grew up around the Roman road we know as the A5, is the birthplace of the Welsh language. The man who championed it and modernised it was Sir John Morris-Jones, professor of Welsh at Bangor University. He lived in Llanfairpwll. I passed his little red house on the High Street. How proud he'd be to know that 76% of young people on Ynys Môn have Welsh as their first language. It's compulsory in schools up to GCSE level. The model was recently studied by a deputation from the Irish Republic, anxious to preserve Gaelic.

Further down the High Street, I came to the Toll House, designed by Thomas Telford to collect charges for horses, mules and wagons travelling on the old A5. It's now the headquarters of Llanfairpwll Women's Institute which is where the WI movement began. Not many people realise that Britain's first ever meeting took place in Llanfairpwll.

They've created a WI museum within the Toll House. The Institute actually saw the light of day in Canada in 1897. Sixteen years later, Mrs Alfred Watt (women clearly took their husband's *christian* names in those days!) came to London to promote the W.I. The response was tepid until Mrs Watt was invited to address students at Bangor University. The official who sent the invitation happened to live in Llanfairpwll. He also arranged for a group of women from the village to meet Mrs Watt and form Britain's first W.I. That was during the First World War in 1915. Calendar Girls were only a matter of time!

Continuing my walkabout, I came to the 90ft high Marquess of Anglesey column which soars above the treetops. It's a tribute to the Right Honourable Henry Paget who lost a leg at Waterloo. How careless. It's said that on noticing the missing limb, the marquess declared: 'By God sir, I've lost my leg!' upon which the Duke of Wellington replied: 'By God, sir, so you have!' (They had a nice line in repartee.) Henry's prosthesis is on display. It's called 'The Anglesey Leg'.

I bypassed this peculiar relic and descended a footpath to St. Mary's Church – the one included in the village name. Alas, I saw no sign of white hazel, but could imagine what they meant by 'the swirling whirlpool'. The path leads down to the sea and a fine view of Britannia Bridge. There's a deep and dangerous stretch of eddying water not far from the bridge. Before the Britannia was opened in 1850, people either waded across the Menai Straits between hazardous sandbanks or took the ferry when it was running. Seventy nine passengers drowned when a ferry capsized in the 1600s.

Picking my way over rocks and seaweed, I met a man with a bucket. He was looking for velvet crabs – ideal bait for catching sea bass. Towering above us was a forlorn statue of Lord Nelson gazing across the water to Plas Newydd, the ancestral home of the Marquesses of Anglesey. The statue, mounted on a rock, was plonked on the shoreline by the son of the first Marquess as an aid to navigation. It looked oddly out of place at low tide. At high tide, the plinth is submerged.

The sun made a brief appearance. Nearby, a young woman sat on a rock reading her novel. She told me:

'I love this coastline. Just to sit and be quiet. I feel sorry for day-trippers who pour into the shopping mall. They don't know this place exists. Just as well really.'

The village is beautifully situated on the edge of Anglesey and the Menai Straits.

My return route to the village centre took me past a charming white cottage sitting close to the water's edge. Along with two more properties, it's all that's left of Pwllfanogi, once a busy shipping village in its own right. More recently, the house was the home of Sir Kyffin Williams, one of the great figures of Welsh art in the second half of the 20th century. His brown-cream-grey landscapes of North Wales have a brooding muscularity about them. Among others, Rolf Harris is a big fan.

That, in a nutshell, is the village of St.Marys-church-in-a-hollow-of-white-hazel-near-the-swirling-whirlpool-of-the-church-of-St.-Tysilio-with-a-red-cave. If you think the name is a trifle long-winded, imagine this: the longest place name in the world is Krungthepmahanaconboworn…(etc.) in Thailand. It has 152 letters. Runner-up is Taumatawhakatang…(and so on) in New Zealand, which contains 105 letters. All of which makes Llanfairpwllgwyngyllgogerychwyrndrobwllllantysiliogogogoch child's play.

Left to right: The cottage of artist Kyffin Williams; The Britannia Road Bridge to the Welsh mainland; What's Nelson doing here?

IN GIANT'S FOOTSTEPS

Milton Keynes Village

Buckinghamshire

You don't need me to tell you about Milton Keynes. Picnickers around the pond; sheep grazing in the pasture; a glimpse of thatched cottages through a gap in the horse chestnut leaves. And so on.

No, not *that* Milton Keynes. This is the ancient version, now officially called Milton Keynes Village to distinguish it from the metropolis which stole its name. This is where the 21st century meets 1265. Apart from a section of cycle track, the spirit of Milton Keynes makes no impression on Milton Keynes Village, even though it's within spitting distance. The village is an oasis in Legoland. A diligently-tended time-warp complete with twelfth century inn, Norman church, several grade two listed cottages and a village green fit to grace Lords. For all that, the village is devilishly difficult to locate. You might stumble across it if you're lucky. It's not on the map and there are no signs until you arrive. Hardly anyone does, because hardly anyone outside the immediate vicinity knows that Milton Keynes Village exists. They don't believe you when you tell them.

It was different in 1967 when the government gave the go-ahead for a new town on prime Buckinghamshire farmland. The village was the only Milton Keynes in town – if you see what I mean. Consequently, it was inundated by frustrated lorry drivers hauling biblical quantities of steel and cement round and round the green and wondering where they were supposed to dump it.

'Not here you fools!' screamed the locals. 'It's the New Town you want. Just follow the bulldozers.'

Such an easy mistake to make. Without warning or explanation, the Development Corporation ignored three existing towns, Stony Stratford, Bletchley and Wolverton, turned its nose up at fourteen other villages inside the 'designated area' and adopted the name Milton Keynes. (The original inhabitants should have copyrighted it!) A misguided civil servant spread the word that the village was named after the poet, John (*Paradise Lost*) Milton and the economist, Maynard Keynes. It would therefore lend Britain's newest and most adventurous project the grandeur it deserved. For the record, the original name of the village was Middleton Kaynes – so he was wrong on both counts.

The parish was part of one estate for 300 years, latterly bought by the Merchant Venturers of Bristol who had eyes on its mineral and quarrying rights. The M1 was imminent! The Merchant Venturers sold the village lock, stock and barrel to the Milton Keynes Development Corporation, who in turn sold the cottages and built a small estate next-door. George Marvin, an 83-year-old former farm manager is one of the few remaining fixtures from that time. He was promised the chance to buy his 330-year-old cottage from the Merchant Venturers at a reduced rate, only to find the MKDC had already stepped in. His daughter eventually bought it for him for £52,000. George went from devastation at the loss of his livelihood and horror at the prospect of years of major construction to:

'Actually, I like having Central Milton Keynes so close. All the facilities are on hand and the village keeps its character.'

And it's all only a stone's throw from the giant metropolis that stole its name.

I can see his point. The combination of rural calm (despite the low hum of the M1) and the best-equipped large town in the UK is hard to beat. Milton Keynes proper offers the famous Snowdome, a professional football club with a modern stadium and the most successful theatre outside the West End, as well as hotels, shops, cinemas, restaurants, nightclubs – and sporting opportunities to suit every persuasion. The Redway cycle track is a huge bonus. It leads villagers half a mile to Willen Lake, once a gravel quarry but now a sailing and wildlife centre.

'We've got it made,' said Phil Gepfert, a builder who lives in Bird Cottage (1240), the oldest house in Milton Keynes Village. 'This is the best place for kids to grow up. It's a parents' paradise.'

If you tell people that Milton Keynes is an historic village, where cottages have roses round the doors, they'll never believe you.

I get the feeling that Geoff Dawe, a retired television producer at BBC's Open University unit in Milton Keynes – MK as it's affectionately known – can't quite believe his good fortune either. After a few years commuting from High Wycombe, Geoff and his wife, Joy fell upon Ivy Cottage, another thatched gem in this hidden village. They now run the Heritage Centre from their delightful home.

None of this may sound like the Milton Keynes you imagined. That's because it isn't. Visit *The Swan Inn* for lunch one day and see for yourselves – if you can find it!

Below: Milton Keynes village is arguably England's best-kept secret.

PORT IN A STORM

Mousehole, Cornwall

Padstow and St. Ives are full of charm, but Mousehole (pronounced Mouzel) feels like the *real* Cornwall to me. Dylan Thomas described it as 'the prettiest village in England.' I think that does it a disservice. 'Pretty' wasn't the first adjective that sprang to mind as I squeezed my car into a small space inside the harbour wall. It's too rugged and gutsy to be pretty. Quaint, yes and colourful, with its granite houses covered with lichen. A couple of fishing boats were just returning. Only seven of them operate out of the village today.

It's where men have traditionally brought home the mackerel and kept watch over its storm-battered shore and women have fed them, brought up their kids and done their bit to keep the Cornish language alive. On Tom Bawcock's Eve, December 23rd, they bake Starry Gazey Pie to celebrate the exploits of a lone fisherman who, driven by the cries of starving children during a time of famine, defied the gales and caught enough fish to last Mousehole the whole of Christmas week. His only companion on the voyage was said to be a cat. It spawned a children's book, *The Mousehole Cat* about which, more in a moment.

Judging by the stampede when the pie's served at *The Ship Inn*, the famine hasn't entirely gone! Starry Gazey Pie, with the heads and tails of pilchards poking out of the crust, is offered free of charge. First come, first served. Donations go to the lifeboat station. Melanie Matthews, the new landlady, was amazed:

'It's a real scrum. Getting a slice of the pie is like a rite of passage. Some villagers have tried for years but can't get near the food.'

Michael Buttery is a case in point. This local fisherman, artist and author has consistently failed to get his hands on the pie for 40 years! They call him 'Butts' and he's now in his 78th year. He recently wrote and published the definitive story of the village, *Mousehole, a Documentary History*. Butts is as crusty as the pie – not only because he can't get any – but because he resents so-called folklorists who trot out the legends of Mousehole without knowing the facts. It took him 50 years to complete his book which runs to 366 pages. Why that long?

'I went through hundreds of logs and official records. You can't rely on hearsay. Many of the stories people tell you aren't true.'

'Like the legend of the cat?'

'Precisely. Cats have nothing to do with it. They don't like water anyway. Yet two ladies from the village made money from the book. It's apocryphal.'

Oops. Poetic licence. He also debunks the commonly held belief that Mousehole derived its name from a nearby cave:

'Utter rubbish!'

Butts' research concludes that it's from the Arabic mozel or mossel, meaning a place of fresh water. He says the earliest traders were Phoenicians and Syrians, attracted by Mousehole's small rivers, unpolluted as they were by the 'tin streaming' industry.

Two reports he *doesn't* challenge are the Torrey Canyon disaster of 1967 and the Penlee Lifeboat disaster of 1981. Sixteen people were killed in the latter – eight of them volunteer lifeboatmen from Mousehole and district. On December 19th, four days before Tom Bawcock's Eve, all village lights are switched off to commemorate their bravery. As for the Torrey Canyon, it seems that several barrels of oil still sit on the seabed. According to Butts, the huge spill which killed thousands of seabirds and the badgers and foxes that ate them, could erupt again.

And so to Dolly Pentreath, bless her heart. It won't surprise visitors to this craggy fishing port that the embers of the Cornish language can be traced to its narrow streets. A survey in 1773 pinpointed an old woman called Dolly Pentreath as the last fluent Cornish speaker. She was a fisherman's daughter and spent much of her time in Penzance, selling his catch. Her cries were in Cornish – the only language she knew. There's a blue plaque in Mousehole immortalising Dolly. Her gravestone carries an epitaph in Cornish and English:

'Coth Doll Pentreath cans ha Deau
Marow ha kledyz ed Paul plea
Na ed an Egloz, gan pobel bras
Bes ed Egloz-ha coth Dolly es.
Old Doll Pentreath, one hundred ag'd and two
Deceas'd and buried in Paul Parish too
Not in the church with people great and high
But in the churchyard doth old Dolly lie.'

Left: In many ways, Mousehole is the essence of Cornwall. The last fluent Cornish speaker is immortalised here.

GLUB, GLUB, GLUB

The flooded villages of Rutland

The names no longer roll off the tongue. Middle Hambleton, Nether Hambleton and Normanton. They haven't for more than forty years. Centuries of quiet, agricultural existence were brought to a close by boffins with a map and a pen. Ethnic cleansing? On a tiny scale, but then wiping villages off the face of the earth is legitimate if a government minister says so.

Poor old Normanton disappeared twice. And yet the sign remains. The Lord of the Manor first razed it to the ground in the 1700s. He wanted more parkland, no doubt to entertain his hunting friends. The estate workers who lived there were summarily dispatched to nearby Empingham. Then in 1970, Normanton was sacrificed for Rutland Water. Europe's largest man-made lake was built to irrigate the growing conurbations of Northampton, Peterborough and Corby.

The reservoir was as large as Lake Windermere. It consumed the valley of the little-known river Gwash, inundating 3,100 acres of farmland. It's twenty five miles around the perimeter. I know, I've cycled it a couple of times. Like it or not, the Lake District had arrived in the East Midlands. Goodbye Normanton, Nether Hambleton, Middle Hambleton and part of Empingham. Hello sailors – literally.

I'm a fan of Rutland Water. It has given Britain's smallest county a USP. Who'd have predicted that landlocked Edith Weston would one day have a sailing club? Who could have foreseen that Hambleton would benefit from being closed off on three sides and thereby marooned on a peninsula? The magnificent Hambleton Hall is a blue chip hotel which attracts international diners to its lakeside tables. Just getting there is an experience.

And who'd have thought Whitwell would be twinned with Paris? Patrons of *The Noel Arms* who dreamed up the absurd notion over a few draughts of Ruddles, were permitted to erect a name board on the Oakham to Stamford road, confirming that the French capital and a hamlet on the north shore of Rutland Water are indeed joined at the hip. Paris probably doesn't even know.

Trout fishing, cycling and windsurfing have all contributed to the metamorphosis of Rutland from an anonymous corner of England to a major tourist destination. They sell timeshare lodges at Barnsdale Country Club on the shore of the reservoir. In early September, Uppingham School's bedrooms are commandeered for the weekend by backpackers with binoculars as the annual Rutland Bird Fair hits town. It's the biggest ornithological event in the country, reflecting Rutland Water's importance as a breeding ground for generous colonies of waterfowl, not to mention ospreys.

It's a win-win situation. The local economy has boomed. New businesses have sprung up. Lovers of wildlife and water sports have unlimited opportunities. Anglian Water's investment is a big success story. Except, that is, for a handful of farmers and farm labourers whose villages were flooded and whose livelihoods were taken away. Who remembers them any more? The small amount of compensation they received took little account of the emotional damage they suffered.

Out on the reservoir, I admired the courtship displays of great crested grebe as we chugged along in the tourist boat, Rutland Belle. It was hard to imagine that as recently as 1970 tractors ploughed the soil fifty feet beneath us. As if to underline that point, we sailed past an underwater tower peeping out of the water like an overgrown periscope. The tower descends to the bed of the reservoir and is designed to monitor water quality. I assume there's a lift to the basement. I've often wondered if there's anything to be seen down there. The remains of a farm? A church tower or two? I guess it's too dark.

Thanks to the wet spring and summer, water levels were high. Ahead of us was the mysterious St. Matthew's Church. It appeared to be floating. A watery church without a village. This grade-two listed building is the one true reminder of a previous civilisation. It belonged to the Normanton estate and (apart from his lordship's stables, which have been turned into hotel bedrooms) is all that remains of a once proud community. We should be grateful for *that* small mercy.

The church survived the deluge by the skin of its teeth. It was deconsecrated in 1970 because the floor was below the proposed water level, making it unusable as a place of worship. It had to go. Only a public outcry saved it from the bulldozer. Anglian Water then filled the lower half with stones and rubble and installed a concrete cap below window level. Consequently we have the top half of a church perched elegantly on an embankment. It's now a museum, telling its own story. It also has a wedding licence. When the sun sets on the reservoir, painting its stone walls a golden shade of bronze, St. Matthew's looks its best. It's Rutland Water's quirkiest landmark.

I can tell you very little about Middle and Nether Hambleton except that the Jacobean Old Hall which once stood in the heart of Middle Hambleton, now teeters on the brink of immersion! The rest of Middle H. and the whole of Nether H. have vanished without trace.

By contrast, their big sister, Hambleton, has gone from strength to strength. Mediaeval ironstone cottages with elevated views of the reservoir could persuade you that the landscape has always been like this. Man is very good at covering up the traces. Much as we choose to ignore it, a great deal of Britain's countryside is artificial. Man made the forests, the fields and most of the lakes.

Rutland property prices pre-1970 were among the lowest in England. Post-reservoir, they're comparable with the Cotswolds! Hambleton's a prime example. How many villages of its size can boast *two* gourmet eateries? Opposite Hambleton Hall is the delightful *Finch's Arms*, another historic building where Sunday lunch goes on until early evening if you're lucky enough to get a table. One of the village curios is an old 'B' road that used to link Hambleton to Manton and Uppingham. It now comes to an abrupt end in the reservoir. One or two motorists must have had a nasty surprise. The vanishing road is now a landmark.

All of which is little consolation to folk who lived and worked in three submerged villages. To add insult to injury, they also had to put up with Leicestershire stealing Rutland's identity during England's ridiculous boundary changes of 1974. Rutlanders are stubborn though. They refused to accept Leicestershire as an address and kept their county signs regardless. In the end, they triumphed. Rutland was restored as England's smallest county. Quite right too! It adds credibility to their motto, *Multum in Parvum* – a lot in a little, or if you like, big things come in small packages.

The half-submerged St Matthew's Church is a striking reminder of a previous settlement. Rutland Water engulfed the rest of Normanton village.

THE LONGEST-RUNNING SOAP

Port Sunlight, Cheshire

What would William Hesketh Lever say if he could see what's happened to his village. Two thirds of the houses he built for workers at his soap factory have been sold to the highest bidder and responsibility for the rest has been offloaded to a Trust. What's more, a small block of (dare I say it?) flats has appeared on the skyline.

Above: Port Sunlight: the dream of a a philanthropist or a control freak?

It's not as bad as it sounds. To the casual eye, Port Sunlight looks the same as it did in 1925 when W H Lever, aka Lord Leverhulme passed away. Graceful avenues lined with lime trees; stylish Victorian homes in a multitude of designs; neatly manicured verges; statues and fountains. Although this son of a Bolton grocer was busy building his global empire, he took an intense personal interest in the development of Port Sunlight. He handpicked thirty architects to give it as much variety as possible. He went through their plans with meticulous care, declaring:

'It is my hope…to build houses in which our workpeople will be able to live and be comfortable…in which they will learn that there's more enjoyment in life than in the mere going to and returning from work, and looking forward to Saturday night to draw their wages.'

It's true, George Cadbury had already started his Bournville project, but he was copying Lever's example. Port Sunlight became an instant hit. It was named after the company's most successful product, Sunlight, a bar of soap which changed the nation's washroom habits. The village had its own port on the Mersey. What I didn't know until I visited the Wirral is that William Hesketh simultaneously transformed an existing village three miles away. Thornton Hough receives little publicity but is arguably *more* charming. His lordship lived there, at Thornton Manor.

I expected to be blown away by Port Sunlight. Instead, it left me subdued. The drizzle didn't help. I admired the houses. I appreciated the landscaping. But something wasn't right. It felt like an upmarket estate. The roads led nowhere in particular. There was no hub, no street life. There are no shops. It slowly dawned on me what the problem really was – rather than *evolve* like most communities, this one arrived overnight. Bang! *Everything* in Port Sunlight was 125 years old – give or take a couple of months. History was shared equally.

The Tudor Rose Tearooms provided a welcome burst of vitality. Most of it came from the owner, Diane Forward who ran a Liverpool-based road haulage business with her husband until this opportunity came along. She didn't pull any punches:

'I took one look at Port Sunlight and fell in love. I wouldn't *live* here though. Sometimes I imagine the houses are just facades. No-one seems to go in or come out. When I wake up in Liverpool where I live, I *know* which day of the week it is. In Port Sunlight, I can't tell the difference between Sunday and Monday!'

By way of contrast, Maria McNally who manages *The Bridge* public house, would like to stay here for good:

'You have to buy into the concept. Some say Lord Leverhulme was a great benefactor – others say

The village became an instant hit. Employees at the soap factory could hardly believe their good fortune.

he was a control freak. Owning all the houses and collecting rent from everyone he employed was a 'win-win' situation. But he certainly created something special.'

It's curious that Port Sunlight has a pub. Lord Leverhulme was teetotal. He built *The Bridge* as a temperance hotel. Under pressure from the workforce, he agreed to a referendum: should the hotel be turned into an alehouse? The 'yes' vote was overwhelming.

At one time, 14,000 worked at the factory. Only 900 homes were built so those who missed out went on the waiting list. Today, the workforce is down to 1,000. Most of them live outside the village. Unilever, as the company became, decided in the 1990s to divest itself of its property portfolio and concentrate on the core business. Trustees control the 265 rental properties that remain.

Port sunlight inspired Cadbury's to build Bournville in a similar style.

There are strict rules for owners *and* tenants. They are not permitted to paint the outside of their houses or cut the lawns. The Trust does that. No 'For Sale' signs can be displayed and Sky dishes must be concealed. This is a throwback to the William Hesketh era, but the benefactor/tyrant would have been appalled to know that a block of apartments has appeared on the outer edge of Port Sunlight. You can argue that apartments are a necessary fact of life, or you can take William Hesketh's line:

'All tenement dwellings – flats and such devices for crowding a maximum amount of humanity in a minimum amount of ground space, are destructive of healthy life.'

The Tudor Tearooms.

Well, he got a lot of things rights and Port Sunlight was a courageous experiment in social engineering. I enjoyed half an hour at the tearooms, but I left the village with the overriding feeling that there's one vital element of a village you can't design, even with 30 architects on the case. It's called soul.

SPLIT PERSONALITY

Purton, Gloucestershire

The river Severn holds a strange fascination for me. Its length and scale are unmatched in England. It's both treacherous and compelling.

The river provides a living for a small band of salmon fishermen who catch them in traditional putchers or lathe nets. In March when baby eels (elvers) materialise in millions, it becomes a cauldron of anticipation as legitimate netsmen come to blows with nocturnal poachers in an unholy scramble for the best beats. The Severn also produces the world's second-largest tidal bore which surges up the estuary with awesome power, carrying surfers as far inland as Tewkesbury.

The bore begins life at Purton, a delightful hamlet north of Sharpness where river current meets incoming tide head-on. When I first dropped by, in 2001, I received a robust riverside welcome and a velvety pint of the local brew from Ted Lord, celebrated licensee of the *Berkeley Arms*. It's a farmhouse-cum-tavern belonging to the Berkeley Estate. Ted was farmer-cum-landlord. The pub had no frills. Its appeal consisted of a comfy old settle by a big log fire and an uninterrupted view of this mighty river.

I returned to Purton this year to find, sadly, that Ted was no longer with us. The *Berkeley Arms* looked deserted and forlorn. Ted's widow, Wendy opens up only when the mood takes her. The tenancy agreement stipulates that she sells (or gives away) a barrel of beer each month. I could only assume she'd

Left: Villagers at Purton West can see the church of St John the Evangelist at Purton East across the quicksands but it would be a 30 mile trip to drive to evensong!

already discharged that duty because there was nothing doing while I was there. Undeterred, I set off along the towpath of the Gloucester and Sharpness Canal to re-acquaint myself with Purton's major attraction – the Boat Graveyard.

The midday sun picked out the wooden carcasses of thirty vessels half-buried in the bank. It looked like the aftermath of a water-borne pile-up. The stricken boats included the 'Katherine Ellen', impounded in 1921 for running guns to the IRA. Further down the bank were two steel and concrete hulks built during the Second World War. The explanation for this apparent crash scene is that in the early 1900s, river authorities decided to run a number of vessels aground to reinforce the narrow strip of bank between the river and the Gloucester and Sharpness Canal. Without it, the two waterways were in danger of becoming one.

I walked between the wrecks with Paul Barnett from the Friends of Purton, a group of volunteers who look after the site. It's not an official tourist attraction and there's no entry fee. In fact, the deceptive nature of the terrain makes it a slightly hazardous experience. Boats were towed out of Sharpness docks on a high spring tide and encouraged to accelerate into the bank at full speed. Once they were embedded, holes were created in the hulls so that silt would cement them further into place. Ingenious!

However, the most curious thing about Purton is that there are *two* of them. It's not a case of double vision. The second Purton stared back at me from the far bank. It was a small cluster of white buildings around the coastal railway line. Technically it's Purton (West), separated from Purton (East) by half a mile of water. But there's no way of getting across other than by private boat. By road, it's thirty miles up the estuary to Gloucester and down the other side – not a popular journey. It's anyone's guess why the village grew up like this. Ferry contact between the two halves was possible for 600 years until 1879 when it was usurped by the Severn Railway Bridge. Some brave souls attempted to walk across but several, including a lathe fisherman who thought he knew the currents, were caught in the quicksand.

Now the railway bridge has gone too. It was demolished in 1960 after two tankers, one carrying oil and the other petrol, collided with it in thick fog. The vessels exploded, killing five of the eight crewmen and blowing the bridge to pieces. Thankfully there wasn't a train crossing at the time. At low tide, the wreck of the oil tanker is visible, sitting in the riverbed halfway between Purton and Purton. It provides a grim backdrop to the boat graveyard.

The two Purtons have therefore lived apart for more than half a century. Indeed, two entire *banks* of the river have lived apart. They can see each other but it's too far to wave. The only thing connecting the east and west bank is the Severn Road Bridge, carrying the M4 to and from South Wales. With the exception of church-goers at Purton (West) who can *see* St. John the Evangelist across the quicksands but can't attend evensong without a major excursion, nobody appears fazed by the village with a split personality. At least one family, the Woodwards, are *grateful* for it. They were torn apart centuries ago by a feud over the ownership of a cow. Half the clan took the ferry to the other side, never to return. The rest were happy to see the back of them. I can't swear to it, but I'm told the Woodward name survives on both sides if the river.

Purton's boat graveyard is a remarkable collection of old vessels which were rammed into the bank to prevent subsidence.

NUCLEAR FAMILIES

Seascale, Cumbria

It's a request stop on a quite magical train journey from Barrow-in-Furness to Carlisle. You have to warn the driver in advance that you want to get off. I was the only passenger who did. It provoked some interest in my carriage. A fellow passenger, Julia Lawrence looked at her watch and told me the workers would be coming off shift at Sellafield any moment now. She knew the routine. She had seven years there as a civil engineer.

'I worked in some of the most radioactive buildings in the world but never had a problem. We had blood tests every three months. The safe level of radiation was between four and seven millirems. Mine was just above four.'

Fortunately, the driver remembered to stop and I stepped onto the elevated platform that is Seascale railway station. The place was deserted. Far across the Irish Sea I could make out a forest of wind turbines. Make your mind up, politicians! Is the future wind or nuclear?

First impressions of this small coastal resort were disappointing. Unlike Ravenglass and St. Bees, it's not pretty. They've spoiled the seafront with a car park. There's a café called Pudding Lane, a beauty salon and a Mace general store. That's about it. With awareness of the past disasters of Three Mile Island, Chernobyl and Fukushima, how can people live alongside Sellafield and pretend life is normal? Well, of course, they do precisely that. The threat of extermination has to be put to one side when it's time to collect the kids from school.

You can't actually *see* Sellafield from the heart of Seascale. But you know it's lurking around the headland, waiting to jump out at you like one of those dreadful phantoms on a ghost train ride. Seascale is half a mile from the most feared, loathed and condemned industrial site in Britain. It's also the biggest. Thirteen thousand people work there. That's most of west Cumbria and nearly all of Seascale.

I decided to walk up the hill to get the best view. I asked the only other person in the street – a man walking his dog – if was I on the right track for the golf club. He looked nervous. Perhaps because I wasn't carrying a golf bag.

Above: The village of Seascale has a resigned affection for Sellafield today.

'Why are you going there?'

'To take a photograph of Sellafield.'

'I wouldn't if I were you.'

He shuffled away without elaborating. What could he mean? You can't get irradiated taking a photograph. Or playing golf for that matter. To be fair, his anxiety turned out to be atypical. Most of the suspicion and superstition which surrounded Windscale (Sellafield's original name) in the early days have been replaced by a resigned affection. It comes from local trust in a more transparent management – and the comfort of stable employment.

Gone are the days when British Nuclear Fuels kept everyone in the dark. When a Windscale reactor caught fire in 1957 and eleven tons of uranium burned for seventy two hours, exposing the Lake District to unimaginable panic, the staff were ordered to *keep quiet*. Since then there have been more leaks, fires, investigations into child leukaemia and rumours of radioactive liquids being dumped at sea. Yet most of the people I interviewed wouldn't hear a bad word aimed at Sellafield. And none of them had two heads!

Keith Hunt greeted me at the golf club. He was sent to Sellafield to oversee the construction of the Thermal Oxide Reprocessing Plant in 1990, but chose to stay on. He relocated his family from Blackburn to Seascale and took up golf. He hasn't looked back. Waving his arm in all directions, he enthused:

'Fabulous course isn't it?'

'Very attractive,' I agreed, 'as long as you don't look that way.'

The northern backdrop is a series of dark chimneys, extensive slabs of windowless concrete and an ugly control tower. Admittedly, Sellafield doesn't monopolise the skyline as dramatically as the cooling towers of

Seascale beach was awarded an international blue flag in 2012 and Seaside Award (formerly Quality Coast Award) in 2013.

a coal fired power station. Nor does it spew out the same amount of cloud. But it's more unnerving. The menace within is silent, invisible and unpredictable. And I'm a supporter of nuclear energy! Keith laughed off my dislike of the view:

'I don't even notice it. It's just a factory. I had many happy years there. But if you cast your eyes due west you can see the Isle of Man. If you look northwest you can see across the Solway Firth to Scotland. And if you look east you have England's tallest mountain, Scafell Pike. Where else do you get scenery like this?'

He was right. It begged the question: why plonk a nuclear power station in an area of great natural beauty? The answer is that it had to be by the sea for easy access to cooling water, and it had to be near a railway line. Since the area was steeped in shipbuilding and mining for coal and iron ore, an industrial precedent had been set. So BNFL compulsorily purchased a couple of farms and West Cumberland (as it was) changed forever. Large numbers of unemployed from Workington, Whitehaven and surrounding communities breathed a huge sigh of relief in 1956 when the Queen opened Calder Hall, the first phase of the world's first nuclear power station. A local newspaper, unaware of hazardous times ahead, declared:

'West Cumberland leads the world!'

Until then, few had heard of Seascale, a coastal hamlet with a beach that goes on forever. A beach which, if you believed newspapers of the 1960s and 70s, glowed in the dark and was lapped by the most radioactive sea in creation. In fact, Seascale beach was awarded a blue flag in 2012. It's packed with bathers all summer.

I called at the library to consult a copy of 'Sellafield Stories', the written version of an enormous oral history funded to the tune of £260,000 by Whitehaven Archive and Local Studies Centre. It's the biggest project of its kind in the UK and was only completed in 2011. There are shocking stories of criminal negligence, mismanagement, blatant exposure of the workforce to radioactive materials, and a culture of lies. The librarian Barbara Clark once went to Sellafield for a job interview but won a place at university instead. She has no qualms about living and working in Seascale:

'There's always good and bad about a nuclear power station. Some people here have concerns but we're kept better informed these days. In any case, being close to Sellafield is a good thing. I'd rather go up with it than suffer the after-effects.'

It's a point of view! Her colleague, Beth Dell added:

'The whole of Cumbria depends on it. I've lived here happily for 40 years. We were a little apprehensive after the 1980s leak. We didn't let the children onto the beach, but apart from that, it's a beautiful, safe place to be. They test the beach regularly.'

The tide was out so I walked several hundred yards to where two anglers were catching sea bass for their supper. From here, Sellafield stood out like a bandaged nose. Then so does Sizewell on the Suffolk coast and so does Hinkley Point in Somerset. Coal fired stations are often 'buried' on the edge of conurbations but their nuclear equivalents are awarded prime locations.

It was almost time to say goodbye to Seascale. The 18.32 to Carlisle was (hopefully) meandering its way across Morecambe Bay and would soon be here.

Meanwhile, a goods train thundered past in the other direction. The ground shook. The wagons probably contained nuclear waste. There's a nuclear storage depot at the neighbouring village of Drigg. Or it could be heading for Barrow to be shipped across continents. Sellafield treats spent fuel from as far away as Japan. It ceased to generate electricity a few years ago in order to concentrate on reprocessing other people's waste. It either turns the rods back into fuel by a sophisticated chemical process, or packs them into steel 'casks' and returns them to sender to be stored until homo sapiens works out what next. Extraordinary though it sounds, Britain is committed to a new nuclear programme without even understanding the endgame! That *is* disconcerting. Homo isn't always as sapiens as he thinks.

Oddly, the only outward hint of hazard in this hazardous place was a poster next to the children's play area. It read:

'Caution. Adders. Do not touch or try to pick them up.'

It seemed trifling somehow.

Golfers, anglers, swimmers and walkers all enjoy themselves in the shadow of the massive international nuclear reprocessing plant.

LAURIE LEE'S LEGACY

Sheepscombe, Gloucestershire

In the summer of 1995, I was lucky enough to meet Laurie Lee. He was frail and he stuttered. His puffy features suggested a life well lived. Cider was only one contributory factor. Laurie, however, was every inch the romantic poet, treating the English language like porcelain. Each sentence had a cadence; each adjective was carefully selected from the rich thesaurus he carried in his head.

This literary giant who wrote two classic novels – *Cider with Rosie* and *As I walked out one Midsummer Morning* – was mine for the afternoon! We took the hill out of Stroud towards his beloved Sheepscombe Cricket Club which is famously perched on a ridge of the southern Cotswolds. This in many ways is the *real* Cotswolds. Plunging hills and farming folk, as opposed to gentle undulations and antique dealers. Sheepscombe had a special meaning for Laurie. This is where his mother was born and where his fellow poet and drinking companion Frank Mansell terrified the life out of visiting batsmen with his raw pace. Frank was assisted by the crazy contours of Sheepscombe cricket ground. Laurie wrote about him – and it – in *Cider with Rosie*:

'At first only the outfield was visible. Then you'd see the top of Frank's cap and his flushed face and great heaving shoulders until, gradually, like a galleon, he'd come billowing into view and loose his fast, furious ball like the shot out of a cannon.'

Apart from its literary fame, Sheepscombe is notable because Laurie actually *bought* the cricket field so that the crack of leather on willow would forever echo through the Stroud valley. He paid £600 for it in the 1960s. The field – for want of a better word – is now held in trust for the village, although the cricket club was hoping to buy it outright. To reach the sacred meadow, you drive up the roughest, steepest approach to any sports field this side of Kathmandu. Several exhaust pipes have been dislodged over the years.

Above: Sheepscombe, on the southern edge of the Cotswolds is hillier and grittier than the touristic north.

If and when you make it to the roof of Gloucestershire, you're confronted by a playing area Laurie likened to 'the back of a limestone pony'. The pavilion is sited between the animal's ears and the wicket occupies a hanging plateau in the middle before the ground drops sharply into a wooded valley and eventually, the village below. The gradient means that a batsman at the top end can't even *see* the bowler until he's several strides into his run-up. A batsman at the bottom end is likely to see his powerful straight drive stop short of the boundary and roll back towards him. To balance things out, fielders on the bottom boundary have to rely on luck or radar to anticipate the trajectory of the ball struck firmly in their general direction. By the time they've worked it out, it's too late.

It's such dodgy terrain that a glider pilot, experiencing mechanical trouble as he flew over Sheepscombe, once elected to crash land in the woods because they looked safer than the wicket! Laurie played the *occasional* game at Sheepscombe, but was a better spectator. As we admired the bizarre but charming view from the pavilion balcony, I'll never forget his telling me:

'The field is theirs as long as they want it. If they ever stop playing cricket, I hope they'll turn it into a children's sports field in honour of my mother. She was brought up in Sheepscombe. She worked for her grandfather in the Plough. Nobody else could control the rough cider drinkers like she could. This is a village for which I have the deepest affection.'

The same sentiments applied to Frank Mansell. This demon fast bowler who struck fear through the local league, was a lineman for the GPO by profession. Laurie supplied this wonderful description of him in 'Cider with Rosie':

'You never knew where you'd run into Frank. He could be shinning up a telegraph pole or emerging from a hole in the road spouting poetry. He wrote verse about the area he knew and loved – country poetry which was never pretentious. Poetry as rough as a dry stone wall covered with moss.'

Between them, the pair published Frank's anthology, 'Cotswold Ballads' and delivered copies in cardboard boxes to pubs in the area. A week later they called back to collect Frank's earnings and take back any unsold books. There weren't many. Frank and Laurie managed to sell two thousand copies – a remarkable effort. After painstaking detective work, I came across one of Frank's poems in the attic of an old friend of his. It was on vinyl and had been set to music. *When the Rain Falls* is a delightful folk tune, sung by a young woman nobody in Sheepscombe could identify. More's the pity. She had a fine voice and deserved credit, albeit possibly posthumous. Also on vinyl and much the worse for wear was another verse recited by Frank himself. Although it was written in the 1960s, it has a resonance today as second-home buyers dominate the Cotswold property market:

'You say you'll pay ten thousand pounds
For this old house and bit of ground.
You like these hills and have it planned
To settle down on Cotswold land.
Well come you in and sit you down
You would-be buyer from the town
And listen to me while I tell
The reasons why I will not sell.

As we know, Laurie Lee went on to achieve fame, whereas Frank died in relative anonymity – a humble lineman, cricketer and country poet. And yet Laurie secretly envied his brother-in-arms:

'I'd have loved to play cricket the way he did. He was a match-winner. I was quite good in the slips, but it didn't make me popular. I remember a Liberal candidate coming to Sheepscombe to show off. He couldn't handle Frank's bowling. I caught him in the slips – a spinning ball I was grateful to hold onto. The would-be member of Parliament exploded with rage, complaining that people had come to see him score *runs*, not be caught out by 'a peripatetic poet'! He stomped to the pavilion in a fearful rage and smashed his bat on the steps.'

Close to the pavilion is a wooden bench dedicated to Frank Mansell. The inscription is the title of one his poems: 'In Sheepscombe let me lie.' And yet Frank *doesn't* lie in Sheepscombe. He didn't actually live there, so they buried him in his home village nearby. Laurie said :

'Frank might not lie here but his spirit does. That bench is haunted by him. He barracks the players when they're doing idiotic things. Frank's unforgiving phantom, champion man that he was, sits there watching every move they make.'

Frank died in 1979 aged 60. Laurie was 82 when he slipped away in 1997. Sheepscombe misses them.

Below left: Laurie Lee bought the village cricket ground so that the sound of leather on willow would forever echo through the valley. Right: A tribute to Laurie Lee's partner in rhyme and demon fast-bowler Frank Mansell.

WHERE THERE'S SMOKE, THERE'S MINERS' PLANNING PERMISSION

Snailbeach, Shropshire

In case you get the wrong idea, Snailbeach is seventy miles from the nearest coast and there's no sand. Snails, however, are a different story.

It's one of a series of exotically-named villages scattered across Shropshire, a magical county where sheep tend to outnumber people and grass still grows in the middle of the road. None of this, of course, explains the curious name of Snailbeach. Let's split it in half and have a stab.

The 'beach' part almost certainly comes from the Saxon 'batch', meaning a small group of houses. Hence the nearby village of Perkins Beach which, according to legend, was entirely inhabited by Perkinses. Perhaps it still is. At any rate, Snailbeach didn't remain a small group of houses for very long.

It grew and grew, largely on account of an ancient by-law which declared that any miner who, starting from scratch, could build and get smoke to rise up a chimney within 24 hours, would be allowed to erect a dwelling on the same spot.

As it turned out, a group of local lead miners put up a chimney stack in double quick time in the 1850s and built a series of hovels around the base. It was stretching the regulations but the planning department turned a blind eye.

The old Compressor House at Snailbeach lead mine.

Before I attempt to explain the 'snail' bit, you should know that Snailbeach Mine was the most productive in Europe. It raked in a fortune for the Marquess of Bath who owned the village and the mineral rights. Unfortunately, as was the custom with wealthy mine owners, he ignored basic human requirements, preferring to keep the profits rather than invest in safety measures.

A thousand men worked at the mine. None of them lived to enjoy their retirement. One Snailbeach resident, Emily Griffiths told me she didn't know either of her grandfathers. Both were lead miners and both died in their 40s, which isn't surprising when you examine the working conditions.

For a start, dress code was virtually non-existent. In the absence of helmets, the miners wore curly-brimmed trilbys hardened with resin. A lump of clay was roughly moulded onto the front of the headwear and a tallow candle stuck on top. To protect their feet from falling debris, the men bandaged each toe separately – the way boxers bandage their fingers before stepping into the ring. Hence the expression 'toe rag.'

It all went horribly wrong in 1895 when Snailbeach hit the national headlines. A rope snapped at the pithead one frosty morning and the cage crashed half a mile to the bottom of the shaft. In a few seconds, the cage was reduced in height from seven feet to just over twelve inches. Seven miners were crushed to death. Compensation was unheard off. Said Emily:

'The miners working in the mine developed a kind of fatalism. Death was around every corner. No-one was afraid of it.'

What has it got to do with snails? Well, according to Emily, they were introduced by the Romans who were the first to mine lead in Shropshire. And, as I discovered, Snailbeach is crawling with snails. I could hardly put one foot in front of the other without endangering several lives. So what's the explanation?

It seems that the edible snail (*Helix aspersa maxima*) was an important part of the Roman diet. It's quite conceivable, therefore, that the present crop is descended from those which eluded Caesar's hungry battalions. I can find no other explanation for the over-abundance of molluscs. Perhaps Snail-beach is missing a trick. Instead of walking on snails, they could be breeding them for the table. With a name like that, and a tradition like theirs, they have a head start!

CHEESE WARS

Stilton, Cambridgeshire

The curious thing about Stilton is that the cheese was never made here. Nor, apparently, can it be. Europe has decreed that only three counties are permitted to produce Britain's most famous food item – Leicestershire, Derbyshire and Nottinghamshire. These days, only Nottinghamshire does. Stilton, an attractive village just off the A1 (M) near Peterborough, has until recently, been left with the consolation prize. It can claim to be the place where the cheese was first *served*. But they're not giving up that easily!

Stilton became popular at weekly markets in the 1700s when the village/town was a busy stop on Ermine Street, the Great North Road. Cheesemakers from nearby parishes loaded their blue-veined phenomenon onto carts and brought it on country lanes to Stilton, where coach parties travelling between London and Edinburgh devoured it by the hundredweight. One such consumer was Daniel Defoe, who stayed at the *Bluebell Inn* several times while writing *A tour through the whole island of Great Britain*. He adored his cheese, did Daniel.

It was vigorously promoted by Cooper Thornhill, a wealthy landowner who bought the *Bluebell* in 1730 as a kind of branch office for his wool business. The race was on. Stilton – the cheese, that is – in its various forms, enjoyed unprecedented success. Some was made with ewe's milk, some with cow's, but all of it pierced with metal rods to allow air to turn it blue. The three counties vied for trade.

Until I visited Quenby Hall, Leicestershire in 2004, I believed the origins of Stilton could be traced back to Wymondham and the two Nottinghamshire parishes of Colston Bassett and Cropwell Bishop. I was wrong. After showing me around his Elizabethan home, Freddie de Lisle, the lord of the manor at Quenby, leaned back against the kitchen sink and reflected casually:

'Just to think, it was in this very scullery that the first Stilton was made.'

Left: Irony of ironies: Stilton village is not allowed to produce Stilton cheese.

This was dynamite! Could he be serious? If so, why had he kept it quiet for so long? Freddie was deadly serious. He just hadn't given it much thought. I made what seemed the obvious reply:

'Why don't you do it again?'

He smiled and said nothing – for six months. Then I got a phone call:

'You know that idea of yours about bringing Stilton back to its birthplace? Well, we've decided to do it.'

As good as his word, Freddie set up a dairy in the outbuildings, appointed a head cheesemaker, signed a contract with a local farmer to provide the milk – and set off on his great adventure. Quenby Stilton was creamy and delicious. Better, in my humble estimation, than the established brands. He got it into the supermarkets and made inroads in the USA. I'll never forget the day Freddie organised a horse and cart delivery of cheeses to the old *Bluebell Inn*, now called *The Bell*. It was like the good old days. The village of Stilton gave us a great reception.

How things change. In 2011 Quenby Stilton closed down. It had overreached itself. Quenby Hall was put up for sale. More or less simultaneously, the village of Stilton decided it was time to take the bull (or cow) by the horns and go into production itself. The parish council was fed up with Nottinghamshire getting all the glory. How ludicrous, they argued, that the village which gave its name to the cheese should be banned by the bureaucrats of Brussels from making it! Defiant councillors erected a plaque declaring: 'The original home of Stilton cheese.'

It drew a predictable retaliation from Melton Mowbray which launched a 'Hands off our cheese' campaign. I'm not sure why. As far as I can gather, this self-styled food capital of England never made Stilton in the first place. Pork pies, yes, but not Stilton.

And so the battle rages on. Regardless of Melton's warmongering, Liam McGivern, the current owner of *The Bell* inn, began making his own cheese late in the summer of 2012. So far, he does it in the hotel kitchens. It's expected to go on the menu for a trial run any time soon. Brussels, however, refuses to budge. If it's made in Cambridgeshire, it can't be called Stilton. Under duress, Mr McGivern has opted for the name 'Bell White.' (Wouldn't 'Bell Blue' be more relevant?) In the meantime, the original Stilton, produced in Colston Bassett, is still served in the hotel restaurant – complete with a glass of port and a spoon.

THE VILLAGE OF FLOATING SHOPS

Stoke Bruerne
Northamptonshire

If you like fresh air, approach Stoke Bruerne from the south. That's the London direction. Approaching it from the north won't do your lungs any good. I tried it once. Negotiating the notorious Blisworth Tunnel, one of the longest in Britain, was like crawling through a tube behind a chain smoker. Only worse. Diesel fumes have nowhere to go. Boatmen in horse-drawn days who 'legged' it through the tunnel by lying on their backs and 'walking' on the ceiling, were spared the suffocation. Whichever route you take, Stoke Bruerne, a village that owes its existence to the Grand Union Canal, is worth the trip any time of year.

At Christmas, a nocturnal parade of illuminated boats provides a dazzling spectacle. For obvious reasons, sailing after dark is prohibited at all other times. And if Morris Dancing is your bag, the annual summer gala will tickle you. However, to appreciate Stoke Bruerne *au naturel,* any weekend with blue skies will do. Part of the village exists independently of the canal, but all the commercial outlets – cafes, shops, and pubs face the water. There's even a curry restaurant, Spice of Bruerne, in a delightful period building opposite the lock. As is often the way with Indian (Bangladeshi) restaurants, the initial outcry against them subsided once protesters were fed liberal helpings of chicken korma.

I chose a warm Saturday in July. The canal was throbbing. A pleasure cruiser slipped sedately between a gauntlet of craft moored on either side. The *Navigation Inn* was up to its usual tricks, dominating the west bank as dozens of customers spilled onto the towpath to dunk their chips in ketchup and sunshine. It was difficult to imagine that the Navigation was built nearly two centuries ago when Stoke was a major commercial hub on Britain's canal network. Coal and timber arrived; flour from Joseph Ebbern's steam mill was dispatched to the capital. Hard-drinking sailors filled the hostelries and caroused with local maidens. Canals were *almost*

exclusively for trade. To my surprise, the first pleasure boat came along as early as 1820, taking day-trippers around Manchester on the Ship Canal.

I learned this at Britain's Canal Museum which occupies Ebbern's old flour mill on the east bank at Stoke Bruerne. You have to squeeze past assorted bric-a-brac and elbow your way through the ice cream queue to get to the museum. Victorian clothing, boatmen's tools, painted enamelware and model replicas of ancient vessels capture the essence of an enthralling era before rail and road haulage signalled the end of canals. The museum recounts the remarkable story of Blisworth Tunnel. It took so long to excavate a passage beneath Blisworth Hill that the Grand Union Canal was in business five years before the tunnel was ready. To connect the London and Birmingham ends of this liquid artery, they installed a 'horse railway' over the hill until the tunnel was open. After giving it a thorough inspection, Thomas Telford finally declared the tunnel fit for purpose. A crowd of 5,000 thronged the village for the official opening.

Waiting for a boat to emerge from the blackness at the Stoke Bruerne end of the tunnel reminded me of our filming adventure a few years ago. Our giant South African cameraman managed to keep his head down while continuing to film for 45 heroic minutes with the sole assistance of a small battery light. We coughed and spluttered our way through. It also reminded me that two boatmen were killed by an excess of fumes and two more were seriously injured in the tragedy of 1862. Since they've installed an extra air vent, things have improved.

None of this is news to Bob Nightingale, a blacksmith who rents a small brick shed next to the tunnel opening. He hears and sees most of what goes on under-ground, some of it unrepeatable. Bob forges ironware for the National Trust and English Heritage, as well as tutoring school groups free of charge. He cut a fine figure with his Jimmy Edwards moustache and heavy duty, ankle-length leather apron. It occurred to me that the facial hair was a potential fire hazard but I didn't like to say anything. Bob was recently commissioned to recreate an Elizabethan fireplace *à la* 1560s. In other words, no sawing, drilling or soldering. A hammer and the furnace were his only tools.

Left: This is where Thomas Telford connected the London and Birmingham arms of the Grand Union Canal – a massive feat of engineering.

The bridge by The Navigation Inn.

A hundred yards down the towpath, it was as if Vietnam had come to Northamptonshire. The Grand Union Canal was busier than the Mekong Delta. There was a boat selling fishing tackle, another selling jars of confectionery and a third calling itself The Cheese Boat. Yes, Stoke Bruerne has its own floating market. All the stalls were doing reasonable business. I was fascinated to know how The Cheese Boat worked. How did the cheese get here, where did it come from, and how well did it keep? The cheesemonger was Michael Prescott, a former marine electrician from Doncaster who adopted the canal lifestyle seventeen years ago. He and his wife,

Geraldine, alternate between the Grand Union and the Oxford canal. The list of cheeses was impressive. Apart from standards like extra mature cheddar, it included leek and white wine; brandy and apricot; red Leicester with chillies. Said Michael:

'As long as you've got a postcode, producers can get cheese to you anywhere. These are all high quality Welsh cheeses. We have five fridges on board to keep them fresh. It's something different.'

With High Street rates driving small retailers out of business, maybe this a sign of things to come, though it's not easy getting business licences from the Canal and Rivers Trust. Applicants are interrogated at length. Stoke Bruerne has certainly benefitted. It's ages since the village had a shop. Now it has a whole row of them.

Top left: Entrance to the Blisworth Tunnel.
Bottom left: Cheesemonger Michael Prescott runs The Cheese Boat.
Centre: Blacksmith Bob Nightingale's forge is next to the Blisworth Tunnel and warns he can hear every word whispered inside it.
Right: Most of the village of Stoke Bruerne faces the canal because that's where the action is.

SCULPTED BY THE SEA

Sunk Island, Yorkshire

I came to East Yorkshire to stand on a sandbank and marvel at nature's creativity. The following day I stood on a crumbling cliff to witness its destructive powers. Both extremes of the sea's ability to sculpt our coastline were evident within 20 miles of each other. Nature giveth and Nature taketh away.

You can read about the shrinking village of Aldbrough on page 11. Both are part of Holderness, a large beak of land overhanging the mouth of the Humber. Sunk Island is more promising than its name suggests. It's neither sunken nor is it an island. 'Emerging Mainland' would be a more accurate, if less romantic, name.

The village is a collection of solid Victorian homes and farms scattered over 8,000 acres of Dutch-style landscape on the way to nowhere. Approximately 230 people live here but you wouldn't know. There's no shop, school, pub, café or village hall. The church is redundant. Summer is wild and invigorating. Winter is wild and rough. Against that, sunrises and sunsets are spectacular. So is the birdlife. Sunk Island seduces you in a way that's hard to define.

It began life as a sandbar which rose out of the Humber like Ursula Andress out of the Caribbean in *Dr No* – though not quite so fast and only at low tide. That was in 1560, by which time the old Saxon towns of Frismarsh, Tharlesthorpe and Ravenser Odd which once populated Holderness peninsula, had been swallowed by the sea. Sunk Island was nature's way of restoring the balance. A *quid pro quo*.

The sandbar, originally known as Sonke Sande, continued to silt up until, by 1660 it was substantial enough to hold its head above all but the highest tides. A new piece of real estate had materialised. Mediaeval speculators soon found their ambitions quashed. The seabed belongs to the Crown as does anything emanating from it. King Charles I promptly claimed his territory and Sonke Sande, (or Sunk Island) has been Crown Estate ever since. The king leased it to a Colonel Anthony Gilby (for services rendered somewhere) and no-one else got a look-in for 165 years. With a grant from the Palace, the colonel engaged Dutch experts to drain the rest of the sandbank and, as if by magic, Sunk Island attached itself to the mainland.

Right: The sense of space in the landscape around Sunk Island is overwhelming.

I first saw it from the train to Hull, a dash of green and yellow on the far side of the estuary. The yellow was rapeseed; the green was barley. For obvious reasons, Sunk Island is as fertile as the banks of the Nile. The soil is Grade One. Land is very expensive. There was still some travelling required to reach this largely-forgotten part of the East Riding. The number 76 bus from Hull takes an hour to get to Patrington, a delightful village of brick cottages with pantile roofs and a magnificent parish church they call the Queen of Holderness. It has a clock on three sides of the tower, facing east, west and north. The south is timeless because it faced the sea. Not any more. Patrington is where I got off. Buses don't go to Sunk Island.

I approached it in the passenger seat of my host, Jeffrey Robinson's car. The former Royal Engineer was longing to show me around this large but apparently deserted prairie which only became a parish in the 1830s. Winifred Holtby immortalised it in her novel, *South Riding* which was made into a BBC TV series. She evokes the surreal image of Hull-Rotterdam ferries steaming up the Humber but appearing to float across fields. At high tide, it's like watching a block of flats sail past.

Jeffrey's a local historian and author who lives in Patrington but nurses a secret passion for Sunk Island. We drove along Brick Road, a track literally thrown together in the 1840s by pioneer farmers using brick ends. It runs ramrod-straight over drainage dykes and past fields of vivid green.

'Look,' said Jeff, pointing to industrial civilisation on the horizon, 'You can see Grimsby clock tower and all the way to Lincolnshire.'

We came to a crossroads with the old schoolhouse on one side and the disused Holy Trinity church on the other. It's now a heritage centre.

'This is the heart of the village,' said Jeffrey, leaping out of the car with great excitement. 'We called it Sunk *Town*.'

Haha! I looked around for bars, nightspots and a cinema. No joy – but I did find signs of human life. A father and his daughter were waiting by the roadside for a mobile farrier to dry-shoe the girl's horse. Dad told me the family had moved to Sunk Island from Beverley a few months earlier. I wondered why?

'The isolation,' said dad. 'We love it.'

The house prices helped too. He paid £100,000 for a two-bed cottage with stables and an acre of land. That would be impossible in Beverley. Before long, the farrier arrived, puffing and blowing. He'd driven from Pickering – a good 35 mile trip. It was the furthest he'd travelled to keep an appointment. Sunk Island is like that.

There was a notice board by the schoolhouse. It contained details of Sunk Island's annual parish meeting and included an invitation from the editor of the Holderness Gazette for villagers to become roving reporters. He was clearly short of page-fillers. Jeffrey read it and shook his head:

'I did that for a time but they stopped using my copy so I gave up.'

On we moved to the western edge of Sunk Island and a place called Stone Creek. Once Sunk Island had been annexed to the mainland, the creek became an established port with wharves, a weighbridge and a harbourmaster's house. The house still stands. In 1869, fishermen who previously operated out of Patrington Haven moved to Stone Creek when their own port silted up. Today it's home to Stone Creek Boat Club and a colony of seals. The tide was out, revealing rippling walls of mud which sparkled in the sunlight. It made me wish I'd brought my easel and brushes. It also reminded me that this is how Sunk Island began. Mud and seawater are an ever-changing feature of this landscape. You can never be quite sure that what's here today won't be gone tomorrow. That probably explains its appeal.

Sunk Island had certainly grown on me. I'll go back one day. For now it was a cross-country journey to the northeast coast of Holderness to see the less acceptable side of wave power.

Mud and seawater are the ever-changing features of Sunk Island's unique landscape.

AERIAL VILLAGES

Trefor and Froncysyllte, Wales

This is a tale of two villages connected by Britain's tallest aqueduct. They're effectively suspended in mid-air. One of them does rather nicely out of it. The other feels the draught. Pontcysyllte Aqueduct carries the Llangollen Canal over the River Dee and still captures the imagination more than two centuries after it was built. The brochure challenges visitors: 'Are you brave enough to cross it? If so, are you brave enough to look down?' A group of Wolverhampton pensioners were apprehensive as they boarded their narrowboat. As one of them said:

'How do you live up to that? We'll be twenty women with their eyes shut!'

Wales leapt for joy when Pontcysyllte was declared a World Heritage site in 2009 – an accolade which puts it on a par with the Pyramids. Such elevated status, however, doesn't wash with Gethin Morris. He lives alongside the canal at Froncysyllte but can't find room to park his car. Two busloads of tourists rocked up from Scunthorpe when I was there. The coaches occupied all the limited space between the towpath and Gethin's cottage. He was spitting fire:

'They're a bloody nuisance. The traffic's spoiling our village. It used to be nice and quiet. They have no right to park here.'

Gethin rewinds to the 1980s when Anneka Rice helicoptered into the Dee Valley and her TV programme *Treasure Hunt* first drew people's attention to Thomas Telford's extraordinary bridge. He claims Pontcysyllte has never been the same since. I guess that he wouldn't mind quite so much if Froncysyllte had grown fat on the proceeds. Sadly, it's not the case. It has to put up with visitors who contribute very little to the village economy. Despite being close to the water's edge, The Fron Café looked worryingly under-subscribed. That's because Froncysyllte isn't a destination village. It's a turning point for narrowboats heading back over the aqueduct.

Left: Sail between these two villages on Britain's tallest aqueduct, and you think you're flying.

Above: There's nothing between you and a 126ft drop.

Most of the goodies go the way of Trefor, the village at the other, northern end of the viaduct. It has a canal basin offering boat trips and day hire, a waterside pub, a café, a visitor centre – and a car park!

By road it's a mile from Trefor to Fron, as they call it. By canal, it's 300 yards. If you don't mind being 126 feet up in the air with a thin metal rail separating you from the drop, it's a pleasant little stroll. The far edge of the trough is alarming. There's no barrier at all. Boaters on that side stare straight into the abyss. That included me. It was slightly unnerving. The trough's wide enough for one boat at a time. Three hundred yards seemed to take forever, although you can always shut your eyes!

I disembarked at Froncysyllte, the less well-publicised but quirkier of the two communities. The main part of the village sits way above the canal. From the High Street, which is actually the A5 between Shrewsbury and Llangollen, you look directly down onto the aqueduct. The most striking edifice is the *Aqueduct Inn*, known to the locals as *The Yellow Pub*. It's more of a lime green if you ask me – and pretty nauseating at that. They reckon it's the only pub you can see from outer space! And on Monday and Thursday evenings you can *hear* the village hall from outer Denbighshire. It's choir practice. Extraordinary though it seems, little Froncysyllte has produced Wales' leading male voice choir.

It all began in 1947 when they entered singers for the Llangollen National Eisteddfod. Many Welsh choirs were nervous about competing against choirs from all over the world. But not Froncysyllte. I spoke to one of the village's great characters, Den Williams, now 82 but still singing first bass in the choir. It was scheduled to star in yet another television programme about the aqueduct and the choir. Said Den:

'In the early days, it was like a Third Division team playing premiership opposition. We were, and still are, just a community choir. But we practised hard and won Llangollen three times. Then we were signed up by Universal, released a CD and toured New York. We made national TV news a couple of years ago. There was a few bob in it for us but royalties don't amount to much.'

Froncysyllte is the poor relation of the two villages. It's simply where the boats turn around and head back across the aqueduct.

Froncysyllte's choir was twice nominated for the Brit Awards. On one famous occasion, it was only pipped by Paul McCartney who was so embarrassed that he apologised. Universal have switched their attention to *Men Aloud* and the wives of war heroes or fisherman, but Fron's 70-strong choir is still booked up for charity shows all over Britain. Den Williams was 16 when he joined. He has strong views about Pontcysyllte and what it means to his village:

'It was our lifeline. Industry, cinemas, trains and buses were all on the other side of the valley. I used to put my bicycle in the boat and row across the aqueduct to work at a chemical plant in Cefan. As young men we swam in it, cycled it and climbed it. I remember cycling over in a horizontal snowstorm. The only way I could do it was by leaning against the railings as I pedalled.'

He dismisses Trefor as 'not a proper village' because much of it was post-war council housing built to take an overflow from Froncysyllte. Fron itself couldn't be developed because of its position on the side of a mountain. The main industry in those days was quarrying stone for lime burning. Donkeys carried the stone across the A5 and the packhorse bridge over the Dee. It's from this mediaeval bridge that you get the best side-on

Below: This 300-yard masterpiece transformed and enhanced the mid-Wales landscape.

view of the aqueduct. No matter how many times you see them, boats in the air are a compelling spectacle.

The original plan was for a low-level bridge with locks on each side of the valley, but this was abandoned in favour of Thomas Telford's revolutionary idea – a cast iron trough mounted on hollow stone pillars to keep the weight down. Sceptics shook their heads. Telford wasn't the legend then that he is today. The mortar he proposed was made of ox blood, lime and water. It took ten years to build, at a cost of £43,000. When it opened in 1805, it created a navigable link between England and Wales, connecting the rivers Dee, Severn and Mersey. From a commercial point of view, it was as important as Spaghetti Junction.

Along with a dozen others, I chose to *walk* back to Trefor. In an effort not to look down too much, I concentrated on the gentle north/south current which is unheard of in a canal. The reason for it is that via the Horeshoe Falls near Llangollen, the Dee flows into the canal. So 1.5 million litres of water flow across Pontcysyllte every day,

Above: Not many people can look out of their bedroom windows and see a boat pass by at eye-level.

destined for Hurleston Reservoir. That in turn provides Crewe and Nantwich with most of its needs. There was even talk of pumping water from the Welsh reservoirs through the canal system to irrigate the drier, Eastern side of England. Seems a great idea to me but to date, that's all it is.

I confess I marched across pretty briskly and was relieved to get to the other end. The last few yards take you above the last cottage before the basin. It must be strange to gaze out of your bedroom window and see narrowboats overhead. Equally, fish in the trough enjoy the curious privilege of birds flying beneath them.

I could see Den's point about Trefor. And I sympathise with Gethin Morris about the parking problem. When Pontcysyllte was awarded World Heritage status, UNESCO promised funds to build car parks and improve the general infrastructure. It hasn't happened. Both villages lay claim to the aqueduct and both will disagree. Neither Trefor nor Froncysyllte belong on a chocolate box but thanks to geology, Thomas Telford and of course, the male voice choir, they have something very special.

The bosky view from the aqueduct.

WHERE TRUTH MEETS FICTION
Turville, Buckinghamshire

Ah, Turville. Or is it Dibley? This half-timbered, brick and flint masterpiece seems too good to be true – which of course Dibley isn't but Turville is. True, I mean. Not that a coachload of tourists were bothered either way. They poured from the vehicle, eager to be photographed in this demi-monde hovering somewhere between fact and fiction. Some headed *Bull and Butcher*-wards; most made a beeline for the Church of St. Mary the Virgin.

Above: Turville is every film-producer's dream of English country living.

This is the focal point of the Vicar of Dibley series.

'It's just like it is on the telly,' declared one visitor, as though he'd discovered the theory of relativity.

Turville has been on the telly since we've *had* telly. Well before Chief Inspector Tom Barnaby, alias John Nettles made his first arrest. After a few years, *Midsomer Murders* took its homicidal fixation elsewhere, presumably because the population had been wiped out! No sooner had it gone than Dawn French appeared at the village gate waving in another caravan of VT trucks, make-up wagons and catering buses. *The Vicar of Dibley* was here for the long haul. Once more Turvillians were tripping over television cables. Would they ever be left alone? And how did the *real* vicar of Dibley take to being usurped like this?

Luckily, the Reverend Paul Nicholson could see the benefits. St Mary's had never been so full. It grew fat on the proceeds. So too did the village. One of its stalwarts, Wendy Duerden told me that the parish council charged £2,000 a day for filming. Each Christmas, the locals received an envelope containing their share of the profits. In a good year, it could amount to hundreds of pounds. That's not all. A steady flow of tourists was good business for the *Bull and Butcher*. That's not counting the production staff who were also partial to a drop of Brakspears.

I use the past tense because *Midsomer Murders* and *The Vicar of Dibley* have moved on. Turville is every film producer's dream of English country living. It is ridiculously beautiful, quintessentially English – and only 30 miles from London. A windmill gazes down from a ridge of the Chilterns. It was extensively used in *Chitty Chitty Bang Bang*.

I began to wonder if I was in Universal Studios. Was there anything authentic about this place? I spoke to farmer and entrepreneur, Bob White, who was once requested by the producer of *The Vicar of Dibley* to provide cows and sheep for a televised farmyard service. Bob excelled himself. Like a modern day Noah, he turned up at the church door with a retinue of cattle, sheep, ducks, goats and pot-bellied pigs. As the menagerie filed into church, the episode took on epic proportions. But it worked brilliantly. Even the threat of bovine bowel evacuation was somehow avoided. Bob loves the Chilterns but takes a dispassionate view of Turville itself:

'It's not a proper village. There's no community. Most of the inhabitants are weekenders or double homeowners. The resident population is falling off its perch.'

A sadly familiar tale. At least Turville has a school, though the neighbouring hamlets of Fingest,

In a good year, residents get a cheque for several hundred pounds each.

Turville Heath and Skirmett keep it going. St. Mary's is open all hours although livestock no longer has *carte blanche* to wander in and out. I couldn't resist calling at the new vicarage, where the Reverend Jeremy Mais had been in residence for four years. He wasn't here during the 'Dibley Phenomenon' but on hearing that he was Turville-bound, the choir at his former parish sang the theme tune of the TV series at his leaving do. It's a version of the 23rd psalm after all.

I finally made it to the *Bull and Butcher*, where my attention was drawn to a framed newspaper cutting

It's ironic that Midsomer Murders was filmed in this crime-free backwater.

on the wall. The subject was Midsomer Murders. Under the heading 'Murder capital of Britain', it pointed out the supreme irony of programme makers choosing the most tranquil backwater in Britain for a crime series. Neighbourhood Watch only distributes newsletters once a year because there's nothing to report.

The double irony was that a particularly gruesome murder *did* take place in Turville in 1942. According to the newspaper cutting, the licensee of the *Bull and Butcher* shot his wife between the eyes as she lay sleeping. Then he shot his dog before turning the gun on himself. I won't go into the background but I could imagine C I Barnaby getting his teeth into that one. Truth is stranger than fiction.

THE VILLAGE THAT LOST ITS POINTS

Twenty, Lincolnshire

Spin on your heels and the horizon's a straight line for 360 degrees. Nothing relieves the monotony. The A151 Bourne to Pinchbeck highway crosses the landscape three feet higher than the surrounding fields. You hardly see but a vehicle on it. The wind arrives direct from the Urals with nothing to block its path.

Welcome to the Lincolnshire Fens. Big skies and endless sunsets but there's nothing over the hill or round the bend. They don't do hills and bends. The bonus is that flatlands offer you a glimpse into the future. You can see exactly where you'll be in an hour's time! There are few surprises.

However, a village called Twenty is one of them. Likewise the road sign which proclaims in hand-painted scrawl: 'Twinned with the moon – no atmosphere.' At least they have a sense of humour. They? Who? There's nobody here.

Passers-by are a phenomenon. Car-spotting has become the local pastime. They gave up on trains in 1969 when Lord Beeching did away with unprofitable lines. Out went cross-country routes and out went Twenty's tenuous connection with the outside world. The original hamlet only existed as a halt on the Lincoln to Kings Lynn line. Contrary to popular belief, Twenty's name doesn't refer to the size of the population, nor to the number of houses, nor to its height in centimetres above sea level. So how *do* you get a number for a name?

It goes back to 1864 and the coming of the railway. An engineer working on the Lincoln line arrived in No Man's Land with a cartload of track to begin work on the next link. Feeling lost in this green desert, he scanned the horizon for signs of life. Eventually he spotted a small shape that turned out to be a sugarbeet farmer approaching on his tractor. The engineer flagged him down and the conversation went something like this:

'What do you call this place?'

'It isn't a place.'

Twenty

'No, I guess you're right but I've got to call it *something*. We're making a railway halt.'

'We know the area as North Fen.'

'Um. That's a bit vague. My workmates will never find me.'

The engineer had a brainwave. He'd count the sections of railway track he'd laid since the previous halt and call it that. The answer was twenty. It could have been worse. Who'd want to live in a place called Nineteen?

Over the next century, a medium-sized community grew up around the halt which blossomed into a small station. Twenty was on the map. A village had been created out of nothing. Then along came Beeching to spoil it all. The station was unplugged. The engineer's toil had ultimately been in vain.

They've found another use for the station building. It's a double-glazing store. As you can imagine, business has been brisk.

Left: The remains of the old platform at Twenty Station.
Above: Welcome to Twenty – the village with a number for a name.

A DOUBLY-THANKFUL VILLAGE

Upper Slaughter, Gloucestershire

I spent Remembrance Day in an enchanted village. It was a curious experience. The streets were deserted. Smoke staggered from a couple of chimneys; a small group of geese paddled in the ford.

Sundays in Upper Slaughter are like that – and this particular Sunday was no different. Elsewhere in Britain, congregations would be placing poppy wreaths on war memorials and singing lustily in honour of those who perished. Not in Upper Slaughter. St Peter's Church was closed. Workmen were installing central heating. Come the full force of winter, they'd need it. The wind can hit you like flint in the Cotswolds.

In contrast, Lower Slaughter was ready to remember. Parking places were at a premium around St. Mary's Church. It would soon be full. Like most communities, Lower Slaughter suffered in the Great War and lost more of its sons and fathers in the Second World War. Remembrance Day, for all its dark echoes, was a major social event. The last big get-together before midnight mass on Christmas Eve.

At 11.00 on November 11th, 1918, when the howitzers were silenced on the Somme, almost every parish in Britain began to count the cost. To Upper Slaughter's surprise and relief, there was nothing to count. And this in a village whose very name suggested appalling tragedy. Every male who fought in the trenches came back to this Gloucestershire farming community alive and well. It might have been renamed *Upper Survival*. For the record, Slaughter has no macabre connections. It derives from the old English word, 'siohtre', meaning 'muddy place' – quite appropriate since both Upper and Lower are bisected by the fast-flowing river Eye.

For this recondite information, we're indebted to Nottingham journalist and author, the late Arthur Mee. In 1936, after the most painstaking research, he produced a book called *The Enchanted Land*. It detailed 32 villages which came through the First World War unscathed. Arthur christened them 'Thankful Villages'. Then came the Second World War. Remarkably, 14 of those lucky 32 villages *also* went through the 1939-45 campaign without losing any servicemen. To paraphrase journalist Brian Hanrahan, they counted them all out and they counted them all back – twice!

Upper Slaughter was one of those villages. It joined communities such as Allington in Lincolnshire and Coyton in Yorkshire in an exclusive group now known as 'Doubly Thankful' villages. It's one of those extraordinary historical facts which has no explanation.

Consequently you will search in vain for a war memorial in Upper Slaughter. There's nowhere to lay a wreath even if you wanted to. Remembrance Day is unobserved because there are no dead to remember. Instead, on a plaque in the village hall, you can read the 44 names of those 'inhabitants of Upper Slaughter who served in a theatre of war' and lived to tell the tale. It almost demands a service of its own.

A poster on St. Peter's notice board announced that the Service of Remembrance would be at St. Mary's in Lower Slaughter. Anyone wishing to pay his or her respects to soldiers, sailors and airmen who were less fortunate, could do so a mile down the road. On the day I was there, six worshippers from Upper Slaughter took the trouble. Understandably, the small coterie didn't include leading aircraftman, Percy Howse, the only war veteran from Upper Slaughter who was still alive. He was 95 and had moved to a nursing home in Bourton-on-the-Water.

I paid him a visit. He still felt guilty for returning from a war which claimed so many young victims.

In a faltering voice, he told me:

'I had some close shaves but I never told anyone – not even my wife. It would have scared her to death.'

I tried to persuade him to tell me more about his time in Algeria and Tunisia but he went quiet. After a few moments thought, he said:

'No. It's a secret that'll die with me.' And it did.

I returned to Upper Slaughter last November. The ford was too deep for cars but perfect for geese. It was sunny and warm. Autumn in the Cotswolds takes some beating. A man on a wooden seat beside the stream sucked dreamily on his pipe. The footpaths were sprinkled with backpackers but the village itself was empty. I'd come to see if anything had changed. Silly really. Time doesn't touch The Slaughters. There was however a new vicar – Reverend Canon Veronica James who knew nothing about Upper Slaughter's unique selling point before she was posted here.

She's up to speed – literally – thanks to a philanthropic group of bikers who performed a tour of Thankful Villages to raise money for Help for Heroes. The tour covered 2,500 miles and took nine weeks to complete. It was the rehearsal for a repeat performance in 2014 to commemorate the one hundredth anniversary of the beginning of the First World War. By chance, Veronica just happens to be a keen biker herself. She and her husband joined the cavalcade through Gloucestershire last summer. They were presented with a plaque officially recording Upper Slaughter's unusual place in military history. The centenary Remembrance Day service will be switched from Lower to Upper Slaughter to mark the occasion, though sympathisers will, of course, have to leave their wreathes at the former.

There's a bizarre twist in the tale. At the back of Jasmine Cottage where leading aircraftman, Percy Howse lived for 67 years, a stone lintel still bears the scorch marks of a freakish wartime incident which took place while he and his colleagues were away on military service. Believe it or not, Upper Slaughter was attacked by the Luftwaffe on February 4th 1944. Incendiary

Although the soldiers all made it home, the village almost came to grief while they were away.

Remembrance Day is just another Sunday here.

bombs rained on this unlikely target. Houses and barns were set alight. The school too. Farm animals bolted. The village was petrified. One resident barricaded herself into the house – only for an incendiary device to land on her roof. She refused to open the door to the Fire Brigade, believing them to be Germans. Neighbours eventually persuaded her to abandon the house before it burned down.

The most plausible explanation is that a German pilot mistook Upper Slaughter for neighbouring Little Rissington where there was an airfield. At any rate, if it hadn't been for Gloucestershire Fire Brigade that February night, Upper Slaughter's returning heroes might have had no village to come back to.

TIME FOR A CHANGE

Upton, Nottinghamshire
Chislehurst, Kent

These are two communities connected by time – *a man-made device to stop everything happening at once* – as someone once defined it. Upton in Nottinghamshire was my first port of call. I wanted to know why we make life difficult for ourselves by putting the clocks back every autumn.

The neo-Georgian headquarters of the British Horological Institute 'hides' in the small village of Upton in Nottinghamshire. I'd driven past it many times and figured out that 'horological' must be something to do with time. What I didn't realise was that watchmakers and timepiece aficionados from Egypt to Ecuador converge on this elegant stately home to perfect their craftsmanship and salivate over its unique collection of clocks. My visit was the start of a revealing journey.

The key to it was William Willett, an eccentric landowner and master-builder from Kent who battled long and hard to persuade government to introduce a thing called British Summertime. They thought he was mad.

The curator of the *British Horological Institute* interrupted his daily clock-winding routine to point me in the right direction – towards a lonely monument 150 miles away in a Kentish Wood where ramblers are reminded of Willett's legacy. He's remembered as the 'Untiring Advocate of Summertime.' It was here, on the edge of the old village of Chislehurst that Willett would ride his horse on early summer mornings in the 1880s.

While doing so, he noticed that most of the houses had their shutters closed. This seemed a deplorable waste of daylight hours. It triggered a campaign which only came to fruition after Willett's death in 1915. This extract from one of his pamphlets illustrates his passion for natural light:

'Light is one of the greatest gifts of the Creator to man. While daylight surrounds us, cheerfulness reigns, anxieties press less heavily and courage is bred for the struggle of life.'

Noble sentiments. Personally, I've never understood why we turn back the hour hand each October, plunging a darker time of year into even deeper gloom. I put the question to a Home Office expert but they seemed flummoxed by it. The party line is that children in Scotland and the north should go to school in daylight and that farmers should be able to milk their cows without a torch.

Both arguments are flawed. Schoolchildren who leave home in daylight must therefore return in the dark, so little is gained. As for farmers, their milking

parlours have electricity. Darkness is no longer an issue. Nevertheless, we must 'spring forward and fall back' whether we like it or not. Common sense doesn't seem to come into it.

Imagine the task confronting Willett in the early 1900s as he tried to break through a wall of establishment incredulity with his Daylight Saving Bill. Greenwich Mean Time had been in existence for only 25 years and Parliament was over-protective. It wasn't about to be derailed by an upstart – aristocratic or not. Willett did, however have his supporters. One of them was Winston Churchill who predicted in 1911 that a grateful nation would one day erect a statue to him and lay sunflowers at his feet on the longest day of the year.

Above: Upton Village, outside the British Horological Institute.

He was right about the statue at least.

Support also came from King Edward VII though he had an eccentric way of showing it. With glorious disdain for convention, the regent declared Sandringham a daylight-saving zone and forged ahead with Willett's idea. He ordered clocks to be brought forward an hour in May and told his staff to ignore GMT. Later on, he imposed the same rule on Windsor and Balmoral. Visitors must have been in constant danger of arriving too early or too late.

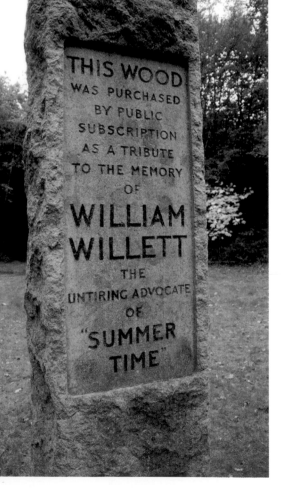

Above: Prickend Pond, Chislehurst.

Top left: The British Horological Institute in Nottinghamshire.

Left: Poor old William Willett died before British Summer Time became a reality.

At long last, our Kentish landowner won the day, albeit posthumously. By a cruel irony, Willett died 14 months before the British Summer Time Act was forced onto the statute book halfway through the First World War. Alas, it still bows to GMT come October. So unless you feel inclined to follow King Edward's example, enjoy summertime while it lasts and pay a visit to Willett's memorial in Petts Wood. The inscription beneath the sundial reads:

'Horas non numero nisi aestivas.' I don't count hours, but summers. He certainly wasn't mad was he?

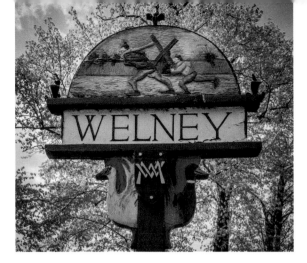

ON THIN ICE
Welney, Fens

The village sign tells the story. A man on ice skates with a windmill behind him and a swan in the foreground. The windmill's a Fenland cliché. The swan refers to the annual winter influx of Bewick and Whooper swans which arrive in their thousands from Siberia.

The skater's less common but equally appropriate. If you chanced upon this unsung community on the banks of the Old Bedford river, you'd have no idea that Welney was the birthplace of British Skating. For such a small village, it produced a remarkable number of top skaters. Necessity was the mother of invention for most of them. In harsh winters, skating on ice was the only way of getting around.

If you were to slake your thirst at the *Lamb and Flag,* you'd be enthralled by the illustrated history of skating which unfolds along the corridors of this pub-cum-museum. It's lined with sepia images of champion skaters who thrilled huge crowds as they raced for prize money across the frozen drains and rivers of the Ouse Washes, the largest floodwater storage area in the UK.

Some would skate to the railway station at Manea, swiftly change their footwear and catch a train to London to race in national events. In the *Lamb and Flag* you can see how they made runners out of sharpened animal bones before metal blades were introduced from Holland.

This was competition at its most raw. Beer barrels marked the start and finish lines. Knowing how to brake around the bends was the difference between winners and also-rans. Distances were guesswork.

A Welney Washes skater takes to the Fens, December 2010.

Sometimes food was the prize. A newspaper article of the time reported:

'During severe winters it is no uncommon thing to see joints of meat hung outside the village pub, to be skated for on the morrow.'

The Fens have intrigued me for a long time. So has skating on canals and rivers. Mainly because I'd never experienced it. There's a feelgood factor about making the most of nature's offerings. While filming *Heart of the Country*, I was lucky to meet Adam Giles, a young adventurer and native of Welney to whom ice skating came as naturally as sledging did to the rest of us.

I was hoping to recreate for television the daredevil antics of legends such as the oddly-named 'Gutta Percha' See, Turkey Smart and his two sons, Fish and James. Adam knew the village history, explained it eloquently and was itching to have a go himself. The weather, sadly, refused to play ball.

We waited in vain for a heavy frost, compromising finally with Adam *rollerskating* on the flooded A1101 and recalling icy winters of the late 1800s when the sport reached its peak. Adam's passionate about his subject but modest about his own ability. He once came third in the Welney championships – pretty impressive to my mind. He played it down. Adam's also passionate about his village:

'Welney's place in history is unmatched. Would we have seen Torvill and Dene if it hadn't been for Welney? Probably not.'

He told me about James Draper-Digby, a Fenland journalist of the 1880s who was so excited by the exploits of James Smart that he created the National Skating Association. With the help of Cambridge dons and a few influential land barons, James D-D managed put this haphazard pastime with its dodgy rules and unofficial records firmly on the sporting map.

Although 'Fish' Smart (so-called because he swam like one) dominated the Welney scene for a decade, it was his brother, James who received the ultimate accolade. He was invited to compete in the Netherlands and became the only British man to win the world championships. It's a record that still stands.

History aside, Welney Skating Club is still very much in business. It is, however, fiendishly difficult to stage the sort of competitions they enjoyed in Gutta Percha's day. Health and Safety rules. The water must be deep enough to cover the vegetation and the ice must be correspondingly deep. The last Welney championships were in 1997. Even the white winter of 2012-13 failed to deliver the right conditions. Said Adam:

'The ice wasn't thick enough. I tried it once and went straight through.'

However, Welney *did* get a chance to revive its glittering past in the winter of 2010. The icy weather persuaded a chartered surveyor called David Lowe, together with his brother and a group of friends, to book rooms at the *Lamb and Flag* and skate 20-30 miles a day for as long as conditions allowed. With only a couple of days' rest, they had a month's worth of sport. David said:

'It was a special opportunity – the first time in Welney history that anyone has skated in November. The ice was perfect. There was no wind. We weren't racing, just covering long distances. Local skaters joined us here and there.'

In theory, global warming will rob Welney of its sporting birthright, in which case, this ancient cauldron of combat will be reduced to museum status. None of us want that. Whether they freeze over or not, though, the Ouse Washes will still attract squadrons of arctic swans and Welney will still be an extraordinary place to visit.

The Bedford River was alive with skaters when winters were much harder than they are today.

FIFTY SHADES
OF BLACK AND WHITE

Weobley, Herefordshire

They have a football ground but it's not called Weobley Stadium. That would be pretentious. They have a cricket ground, a bowling green, a deli, a restaurant, three pubs, a cinema and a theatre of sorts. Come to think, there isn't much Weobley *doesn't* have.

This fact persuaded the *Daily Telegraph*, in conjunction with Calor Gas, to crown it 'Village of the Year' in 1999. It was judged on the wide range of activities in which the population (about 1200) regularly immersed itself – and nowhere else could hold a candle to Weobley. They're still basking in the afterglow of that success. I was introduced to Jo Ware, a farmer's wife who had the foresight to set up Weobley's popular Heritage Trail. Too many visitors seemed to amble aimlessly through the village and miss its landmarks. Jo said:

'If the *Daily Telegraph* came back today, they'd find very little has changed.'

'Oh yes it has,' interjected Marlene Edge, a barmaid at the *Unicorn* (where we were having our discussion}.

'We don't have galas or dances any more.'

Jo conceded the point but suggested that society, rather than the village, had changed. She was referring to the numbing effect of social media sites which eventually cast their spell over Herefordshire, once a Twitter-free zone.

Left: Admiring Weobley's wealth of oak beams, it's hard to believe that the oak tree was once called 'the weed of Herefordshire'.

An advert I noticed in Weobley's parish magazine, *The Magpie* perhaps best captured the spirit of this rural outpost. On behalf of the hardware shop, it announced: 'Loose grass seed has arrived', as though the entire village had been stressing about a bare patch in the lawn.

The shop, incidentally, is run by 79-year-old Ann Preece, not only born and raised in Weobley but reluctant to accept that life beyond its boundaries is worth mentioning. Her hardware shop would make a telephone kiosk look roomy. It's packed with an eclectic mix of light bulbs, rawl plugs – and Haribo sweets.

Ann glossed over the grass seed story as though it was old news. Instead, she wanted to talk about her new boyfriend. I heard the opening salvo then made my excuses and left. Septuagenarian romance wasn't on my agenda. Iconic though Miss Preece undoubtedly was, I had other things to attend to.

What makes Weobley stand out is its black and whiteness. There are no shades of grey. This village is the Jewel of Herefordshire's famous Black and White Trail, a route created in 1987 to attract tourism. Several villages such as Dilwyn, Pembridge and Eardisland are on the trail, but Weobley has the most eye-catching display of half-timbered cottages. They stand at peculiar angles to its gently sloping streets, just as they have since they were erected seven centuries ago.

Hence the larger-than-life carving of a magpie on the village green. Weobley's black and white symbol was created by a Polish sculptor, Walenty Pytel who works in scrap metal. The magpie was commissioned to celebrate the *Daily Telegraph*/Calor Gas award. Although some of the 'white' is distinctly cream or faded yellow in places, the overall effect is enchanting. A company called Border Oak exports replica cottages as far as Japan!

But who chooses to live in this rolling landscape between England and Wales where motorways don't reach and people still point at aeroplanes? Was Weobley a twee, middle-class retirement haven?

'No,' countered Helen Quinlan, a parish councillor who'd drifted south from Flintshire:

'There's nothing twee about it. This is a working village and a farming community. Our infant and senior schools are buzzing.'

Helen had another surprise for me. She personally didn't and wouldn't want to live in a black and white cottage. Why?

'You never know what's inside the wattle and daub. Don't forget, these were peasant cottages built cheaply out of local oak. Oak was called *the weed of Herefordshire*. In the early nineteenth century, a lot of houses fell down.'

The magpie is of course the village emblem.

Weobley is the jewel in Herefordshire's Black and White Trail.

There's always a catch! Thank goodness a lot of houses *didn't*. While getting my head around that disappointment, I bumped into Annie Austin, a middle-aged hippy who flounced into the butchers, hair flowing, cotton shoulder bag swinging. She told me she was a tour operator who spent most of her time in Morocco but kept a house in Weobley:

'I adore the place. It's a great foil for Marrakesh. My London friends thought I was mad wanting a second home here. As soon as they visited, they were green with envy!'

To add to the international flavour of this otherwise self-contained parish, a notice in the butcher's shop urged customers to 'Buy Polish sausages.' The plot thickened when the butcher, a ruddy-faced man with a strong Herefordshire accent told me his name was Julian Kowalewski. Could he be related to Walenty Pytel, the sculptor? This was too much of a coincidence.

As it turned out, there was no connection, but Julian enlightened me about a wartime Polish camp called Foxley which was ten minutes down the road. According to Mr Kowalewski, it was once a small town. These days it's a tree plantation but the huts are intact. Julian's family escaped there when the Germans took Ukraine where they then lived. Yep, I get the drift, but what about the sausages?

'I got the recipe from Poznan when I went to visit relatives. The sausages are spicy and herby. Like to try one?'

I thanked Julian for the offer but opted for a pork pie hand-reared in Weobley. Got to keep the faith.

A NOVEL IDEA

Westward Ho! Devon

It's not unusual for books to be turned into films and plays, but villages? That's unheard of. Westward Ho! is the only place in the world which owes its existence to a novel. Charles Kingsley's blockbuster spawned a Victorian seaside resort of the same name. Fiction became fact.

Rewind to the 1850s. The author stands on a barren north Devon beach conceiving the plot of his seafaring adventure. The last thing on his mind was the rash of hotels and villas that sprang up as a direct result of his novel. He wouldn't have wanted that.

Whether we like it or not, Westward Ho! is in business. It's also the only place in Britain with an exclamation mark at the end of its name (Plymouth Ho! is the name of a waterfront). Yet few of the locals I met had any idea of the village's extraordinary history. Even fewer had read the book.

Kingsley borrowed the title from Thames ferrymen who would traditionally cry 'Westward Ho!' or 'Eastward Ho!' before setting off upstream or down. His book was an instant bestseller. It's the story of a young sailor from Bideford who follows Francis Drake's voyage to the Caribbean, fighting off the Spanish on his way. It contains colourful descriptions of the coast around Bideford where Kingsley took rooms while writing his novel. Here's an example:

'All who have travelled through the delicious scenery of North Devon must know the little white town of Bideford ----- there's a wide expanse of hazy flats, rich saltmarshes, rolling sand hills and the everlasting thunder of the long Atlantic swell.'

What he couldn't foresee was that a group of wealthy entrepreneurs, led by the Earl of Portsmouth, would attempt to cash in on the book's success by turning the 'rolling sand hills' into a pleasure dome Kubla Khan

style. They formed the Northam Burrows Hotel and Villas Company Ltd in 1863 to recreate the flavour of the novel and bring tourism to an under-developed coast. The company's mission statement included this:

'The recent publicity of Professor Kingsley's Westward Ho! has excited increased public attention to the western part of this romantic and beautiful coast. '

The plan was half-baked. It hinged on a new railway line intended to bring holidaymakers flooding from the Home Counties. Having fought off considerable objections by local councillors, the company built its hotels and villas and topped them off with an extravagant railway station. By 1901, the Bideford, Westward Ho! and Appledore Railway was up, but going nowhere. The London link never happened. The unwieldy BWH and AR found itself cut off from the rail network. Its fate was sealed. The line closed in 1917.

Westward Ho! is now submerged by the familiar trappings of a British seaside resort – doughnuts, go-karts and amusement parks. It is the embodiment of everything Charles Kingsley would have hated. Only pockets of its original grandeur remain. The original railway station became a bus station before falling derelict; the Bath Hotel where Victorian ladies bathed in water pumped by a steam engine, was replaced by an apartment block; the Grand Pier was wrecked by Atlantic storms. Touché, as Kingsley might have said.

However, I can report that Westward Ho! hangs on in there. Though possessing none of Bideford's (slowly vanishing) charm, it is blessed with a wonderful two-mile stretch of surfing beach – something the Victorians overlooked. Baring torsos wasn't their style. The village also boasts England's oldest golf club, The Royal North Devon, established in 1864. As for Kingsley, he never once visited the resort and made no secret of his disapproval. Until the Earl of Portsmouth and his cronies moved in, the Pebble Ridge – a high bank of stones and shingle

It's just as well Kingsley's statue is in Bideford - he hated Westward Ho!

which gathers at the back of the beach – was one of his favourite haunts. Kingsley used to pay quarrymen to move some of its large boulders aside so that he could examine the marine life. Hence his thinly veiled horror at the prospect of a tourist invasion:

'Spoiling that beautiful place with hotels and villas, you will frighten away sea pies (oyster catchers) and defile the Pebble Ridge with chicken bones and sandwich scraps.'

They didn't listen. They could see pound signs. Kingsley refused to attend the resort's opening ceremony and resented the use of the name Westward Ho! I sympathise with him. North Devon, in my view, fails to get its act together. With one or two exceptions, a bleak modernity has spoiled its natural assets. Westward Ho! is a case in point. Sorry folks!

Surely it would have been better to resist demolishing or modernising Westward Ho! and leave it as it was – a Victorian folly. Then they could have capitalised on its literary history. Rudyard Kipling went to school there during its brief heady days. The combination of Kipling and Kingsley should have offered plenty of scope.

Perhaps it isn't too late. As I write this, the resort has just celebrated its 150th anniversary. A long-overdue Community History Project was eventually established in 2003 to help the population appreciate the village's strange inheritance, so things are moving in the right direction. There has to be more to look forward to than chicken bones and sandwich scraps.

Westward Ho! still attracts tourists, but most of its Victorian glory has gone.

IDENTITY CRISIS

Winchelsea, Sussex

They love dressing up in Winchelsea. Any pretext will do. On the Sunday I called, the Patronal Festival Eucharist had them diving into their period costumes. On the stroke of 10.30, Winchelsea's mayor, red cape swaying, ornamental hardware glistening in the warm sun, led a robed and bewigged procession of 'jurats' through the churchyard. A jurat is a handpicked member of the mayor's team of officials.

The procession went close to Spike Milligan's grave in St Thomas' churchyard. He'd have had a field day with the pomp and circumstance. Spike lived across the vale at Udimore but asked to be buried within sight of the English Channel. St. Thomas' Church in Winchelsea is multi-denominational, so Spike's Catholicism didn't matter. The only proviso was that his celebrated epitaph, 'I told you I was ill' had to be carved in Gaelic. The Diocese deemed the message irreligious.

Jurats' wives congregated by the church door comparing hats and dresses as though it was Henley Regatta. One of them, with the improbable name of Bren Dunk, whispered in my ear:

'We have a rebel in the village. He thinks this is nonsense and the jurats are a waste of time. He can think what he likes. We love our ceremonies. It's what Winchelsea's all about.'

'So who is the dissident?'

Bren looked sheepish: 'I can't tell you that!'

Left: Winchelsea silted up and was rebuilt on an island by Order of the King.

The chosen few followed the rector's swinging incense burner into church and the Patronal Festival began. A warning above the porch urged:

'Please close the doors to keep the pigeons out.' Pity. They'd have increased the rector's flock! I duly complied.

Let me tell you more about this extraordinary place. Winchelsea sits on Iden Hill looking down at the English Channel. Prime location. But the village has an identity problem. Did I say village? Sorry. I meant 'town' though to all intents and purposes, it *is* a village. Even the official guide-book says so. Here's a sample sentence:

'Visit Winchelsea and you will see what appears to be a neatly kept, well-preserved village.'

Yet 'village' is just about the worst insult you can hurl at Winchelseans. My decision to include it in this book is in itself treasonable. 'We're a town!' they cry. 'What do you mean identity problem?' I'll come to that.

Whatever its administrative definition, Winchelsea's an outstanding collection of (largely) wooden houses gathered around a half-ruined 'cathedral'. It should be re-christened New Winchelsea. The original port lies under the waves. It was obliterated in the fearful storm of 1287. Tsunami's a new word in the English language but not a new phenomenon. Because of the original town's importance to the realm, King Edward I personally came to the stricken community's rescue. He ordered Winchelsea to be rebuilt on an island called Iden Hill. In the succeeding centuries it almost grew into a city. Bigger than Southampton; more important militarily than Portsmouth; second only to London as an importer of wine. From its unique position, Winchelsea dominated the south coast.

Top left: Spike Milligan's epitaph just had to be in Gaelic!

Bottom left: A row of Winchelsea's fine tile-hung houses.

By no stretch of the imagination can that be said today. Winchelsea's high and dry. Not only is it now enclosed by fields rather than water, but it's a job to *see* the Channel. It has a population of 400, half of whom are weekenders. They come and go like the tide which once lapped against its shore. It has a school and a cricket club, though both are sustained from outside. There simply aren't enough young people from within to keep teachers – or umpires – busy. The geriatric factor may be Winchelsea's next problem.

So, you might ask, what happened to King Edward's pet port? Basically it silted up. Even the monarchy can't control the tide. Winchelsea's source of prosperity, the sea, was also its undoing. The easterly drift of shingle eventually clogged the harbour. Ships bringing Burgundy and Beaujolais could no longer dock. Worse still, nature redrew the map. The coast now went *around* Winchelsea. Island days were over. Trade collapsed. People left. Smuggling was the only job in town. Sorry, I mean village! Let's explore the distinction.

By a stroke of luck, or maybe out of sympathy, Parliament made an exception of Winchelsea when it abolished Britain's municipal corporations in 1883. Winchelsea Corporation was and is bomb proof. Big deal? Not really. Although it's entitled to call itself a town and retain a mayor, it has none of the powers normally associated with a town. In fact it has no powers at all. It doesn't even qualify for a parish council, falling instead under the local government auspices of neighbouring Icklesham. Not so much a toothless bulldog, more of a mute canary!

I'm being cruel. As Mrs Dunk hinted, its eccentricity is its charm. When the Patronal Festival was over and the wine had been savoured, eight Supermen climbed out of fancy dress and became Clark Kent again. Among them, Mike Melvin who took a short break for Sunday lunch then reported for duty at the museum. Mike's a cockney who fell in love with Winchelsea and moved here 24 years ago. He's a former mayor – but that applies to most of the male population. It all goes back to the eleventh or twelfth century (nobody's entirely sure) when Parliament nominated a group of ports closest to France to provide ships and sailors in the event of war. These were the Cinque Ports. A curious title considering there were seven of them – Hastings, Dover, Hythe, New Romney, Sandwich, Rye and Winchelsea. Each was expected to provide fifty seven ships with a crew of twenty men and one boy for fifteen days a year. If England and France were at peace, the ships were used for royal voyages abroad. In return, the Cinque Ports enjoyed many privileges, including tax-free imports.

The coming of the Royal Navy put an end to this practice and the Cinque Ports were downgraded to ceremonial status. Winchelsea must have pulled rank to get a mayor and a municipal corporation, nominal though they are. As it turned out, smuggling was endemic. Certain townsfolk were as guilty as the gangs they were supposed to be policing!

Winchelsea was once bigger than Southampton and more important in naval terms than Portsmouth.

That's the history – now the present. It's no good standing for mayor unless you're prepared to pay the price. According to Mike Melvin, a year in office will set you back somewhere between £3,000–£4,000. There are functions to hold, meetings to attend, costumes to buy. Expenses accounts don't exist. Other Cinque Ports mayors have chauffeurs, but not Winchelsea. *Its* mayors live in dread of the Queen dying or abdicating on their watch. They'd automatically become what is called Coronation Barons, required for service at Westminster Abbey. Dread? It's a great *honour* isn't it?

'Yes,' said Mike, 'but it's a hell of a financial burden. The uniform costs an arm and a leg for a start.'

He gave me a tour of the magnificent Court Hall Museum. Unlike most of Winchelsea's buildings, it's made of stone – an indication of the wealth of Gervase Alard, Winchelsea's first mayor. He lived in the building.

'You either love Winchelsea or you hate it,' said Mike. 'Some people think we're a funny lot. We enjoy celebrating what our ancestors achieved, that's all.'

Unless you live in the southeast, it's difficult to imagine what it was like living in Europe's direct line of fire. People were on permanent alert. I'm certain the Cinque (or more accurately Sept) Ports deserved their concessions but it's also true that the government occasionally over-compensated. The Royal Military Canal is an obvious example. It was dug to give Napoleon's troops one more barrier to negotiate, and runs for 28 miles from Folkestone to Hastings. A thoroughly wasted effort. The canal was never used in anguish and has seldom been used for pleasure. It passes through Winchelsea, overgrown, dirty and unnoticed, except by anglers and dog walkers. Since it doesn't connect with the rest of England's canal system, you'd need a low loader to launch a narrow boat.

I left Winchelsea in no doubt that it's a village which likes to think it's a town. That's not intended to be pejorative. Recent campaigns by the Winchelsea Action Group to establish their own parish council have singularly failed. I can understand why a community wants to run its own affairs, especially when its past has been so illustrious – and hazardous. The trouble is that to have a parish council, Winchelsea would have to forfeit its status as a town, however meaning-less that might be. They can't have it all ways. To the unnamed dissident, I'm tempted to say:

'History's against you, pal. Let sleeping dogs lie.'

Top: Is it a village? Is it a town?

Middle: Winchelsea's imposing entrance.

Bottom: Keeping up the standards although the Mayor has to buy his own gowns.

THE VILLAGE OF PAINTED WINDOWS
Woburn, Bedfordshire

We're familiar with the Abbey and the eccentricities of the various Dukes of Bedford. We've been to the deer park and admired the herd of Père Davids. We've enjoyed Woburn's annual Oyster Festival but wondered why it takes place in a village as far removed from the oyster beds as you can get (although it *is* in Beds!)

We're aware of its history as a major north-south *and* east-west staging post and we know that sixteen inns once accommodated passengers and horses travelling by stagecoach between London and Manchester or Oxford and Cambridge. We love Woburn's Georgian high street peppered with trendy shops, restaurants and galleries.

But the chances are that we've overlooked Woburn's most extraordinary claim to fame. The Dukes of Bedford have been hoodwinking us for centuries. Everything isn't what it seems on Woburn's iconic high street. Particularly *vis-à-vis* the windows. If you don't believe me, count how many have no glass in them. In other words, they've been *painted on*. I counted 41 on the high street alone. Heaven knows what lurks around the back! That's far more false windows than anywhere else in the country.

It goes back to the 1698 window tax, but why so many – and why in what must be one of the wealthiest little enclaves in Britain? Surely Woburn didn't need tax dodges? Parliament, you may recall, introduced the window tax under the succinctly named 'Act of Making Good the Deficiency of Clipped Money.' Basically, 17th century Brits took exception to the idea of *income* tax. They thought being ordered to reveal their incomes was a gross intrusion of privacy.

Right: There are three false windows in this photo alone, of part of Woburn's main street.

Don't be fooled by appearances. All is not what it seems on Woburn's high street.

So they dreamed up the window tax. The charge was two shillings per house (just over £11 in today's money) but extra for those with ten windows or more. Despite protests about a tax on 'light and air', it lasted for a century and a half. Needless to say, though, thousands of homeowners found a way around it. They simply bricked up their windows. You can see them on period buildings everywhere. Painting over the brickwork to make them look real presumably served two purposes. One was to preserve the look of the building. The other was to disguise rampant tax evasion – or avoidance. But forty one of them? That's more like a boast!

The assistant at Jackson-Stops and Staff estate agents was astonished when I told her that the building had no fewer than eight false windows, which was possibly a British record. She stepped outside to count them. Four on the front; four more around the side. Yes, I was right. She'd never noticed. To be fair, most of them were on the first and second floors. It must be dark up there.

The one person you can't fool is the window cleaner. As luck would have it, I found one halfway up his ladder and asked him whether it made Woburn an easy place to keep clean. He laughed:

'Good question, but there are still plenty of real windows, believe me.'

'Have you ever cleaned a painted one by mistake?'

'No, but there's always a first time.'

I needed to find out why those mock windows, beautifully painted though they were, hadn't been replaced with the genuine article. The tax was rescinded in 1851 for goodness sake! This proved difficult to nail down. Although several properties have been sold down the years, the majority still belong to the estate. That includes most of the tall buildings fronting the main street. As helpful as they were in the information centre, no-one could shed any light on the continuing subterfuge. Shopkeepers and café owners were as surprised as the girl in the estate agents. Cue Andrew Ian Henry Russell, the fifteenth Duke of Bedford.

The explanation was fairly mundane. Money. I suspected as much. Most of the floors with painted windows were used for storage. That's a relief. I had images of serfs slaving in black, bat-infested rooms. Replacing the pretend windows with glass didn't seem worthwhile. Nobody would even notice.

The lovely irony is that the very wealthy, far from bricking up their windows, had extra ones *put in*. It was a display of opulence – and a considerable boost to the Exchequer. Presumably the eighteenth century Duke of Bedford had three options: follow their example; leave his glass windows intact and pay his dues – or brick them up and paint them to deny the taxman. Woburn High Street gives you the answer.

See if you make it forty one.

SPA GOING SPARE

Woodhall Spa, Lincolnshire

It's harvest time. Lincolnshire's doing what it does best. We travel past mile after uniform mile of razed fields of wheat. A slow-drifting cloud of dust on the horizon indicates another combine at work.

Then, suddenly, everything's green. Trees form a canopy. The smell of hay becomes the perfume of scented pine. I step off the bus into an oasis called Woodhall Spa. Or is it a mirage? In the village heyday, I'd be stepping off the *train* but Lord Beeching got here before me. Lords, ladies, professors and princesses once poured off its platform and into its hotels, believing that Woodhall's healing waters could wash away a lifetime of bodily indulgence.

With the exception of the spa baths and the railway station, the infrastructure's still intact. It consists mostly of elegant, leafy Edwardian boulevards punctuated by grand houses with carved balconies, a luxury hotel, a championship golf course and more restaurants than you'd find in Finchley Road. You'll never see a tractor rolling along The Broadway. I can imagine patrolmen turning them away at the village border. Woodhall Spa might be surrounded by farmland but it's as far removed from the pitchfork as Birmingham is from sardine fishing. Surrey or Hampshire would be a more natural home.

Before exploring its glorious but relatively brief history as a resort, I wanted to see Woodhall's overgrown outhouse of a cinema, called Kinema in the Woods. It didn't disappoint. Although it was the middle of the day, parents and children marched in to watch a matinee for the school holidays. Inside, the lighting was soft and the atmosphere magical. There were queues at the sweet stall. There's talk of a third screen.

Left: Lords, ladies and royalty once sat in deckchairs at the Kinema in the woods.

Peter Scott's shoe shop.

The Kinema, named after the Greek 'kine' meaning film, is a light-weight pavilion built in the 1890s to host bazaars, flower shows and parish council meetings. It once had a verandah from which spectators could watch cricket and tennis played in the Spa grounds. The pavilion's set in thick woodland just off the village centre. When the Spa began to fail in the 1920s, a local dignitary, Sir Archibald Weigall, decided that a picture house would help to offset the recession. And so, to general approval, the village hall was transformed into Pavilion Kinema. The first rows of seats were deckchairs, frequented by an illustrious clientele, including royalty. Safety regulations stopped the fun in 1952. Deckchairs were replaced by traditional seating.

The Kinema is owned by James Green who bought it in 1973. One of his first tasks was to install a Compton Kinestra organ which emerges from under the stage during the interval. These days it's played by the local jeweller, Alan Underwood. He can't make the weekday matinees, but he tinkles the ivories whenever business allows. This iconic movie house has weathered the advent of multi-screen rivals and attracts a devoted following who regularly fill its 400 seats. It has a unique method of back-projection, made necessary by low ceiling supports which don't allow a beam to hit the screen in the usual way.

The Kinema is Woodhall's most iconic building.

James told me:

'The cinema industry was bumping along on the bottom in the early Seventies. A film rep tipped me off that the Kinema was up for sale. The previous owner had fallen ill. I fell in love with the building the moment I saw it. It wasn't doing great business. It needed more enthusiasm.'

James Green was the man to provide it. During school holidays, he puts on a staggering 56 shows a week. His long-time pal, Dave Gilks, was making lattes and americanos when I dropped in. The place was teeming. Dave said the Kinema, or 'flicks in the sticks' as troops used to call it when they were billeted here, was Woodhall's social hub. It opens every night of the year except Christmas. It receives all the new films as they come out. Some customers desert their traditional cinemas in Lincoln and Boston to savour its unique atmosphere.

Victorian hotels were once crammed with wealthy spa clients.

Next to the Kinema is a boarded-up relic of the mid-1800s – a period of unprecedented and unequalled economic success. It was the Pump Room, also known as The Baths. It's been derelict for more than a hundred years. A 'for sale' board's pinned optimistically to its portico. Who'd want such a rambling lump of architecture and what would they do with it? Granted, the 'magical' water is still underground as it always was but accessing it is beyond the wit and wallet of most prospective buyers. The well collapsed in dramatic fashion in 1983. Masonry was sent plunging 650 feet down the shaft. Unless a Russian oligarch rolls into town, notions of a Spa revival are fanciful in the extreme. But you never know. To find out more, I phoned for an appointment with the estate agent, Banks Long & Co.

In Victorian times, Woodhall was hailed as 'A Lincolnshire Buxton' because its mineral springs were rich in bromine and iodine. Whatever your ailment – rheumatism, eczema, jaundice, gout or acne, Woodhall Spa water would put you right. Or so they believed in those naïve and impressionable times. The fact that the water tasted foul was all to the good. This was an age when to be of any value, medicinal potions had to be unpleasant.

The village became an El Dorado. The Lord of the Manor, Thomas Hotchkin, was told of its enormous potential and advised to think big. 'Extend the facilities,' they said, 'Landscape the whole area.' Thus a small part of England's least wooded county was filled with ash, pine and horse chestnut as Woodhall became Britain's first garden village. The opening of a rail link from Kirkstead to Horncastle in 1855 was the icing on a lucrative cake.

I was introduced to Marjorie Sargeant, a former schoolteacher from Newcastle who's produced three books about her adopted home. She described how the cream of British, European and indeed worldwide society came for total immersion. After treatments, these global luminaries would stroll in full evening garb through woods hung with Chinese lanterns. They'd sip champagne at the magnificent Victoria Hotel which charged between twelve and fifteen shillings a day for a room! At its height, the Vic's annual turnover was £25,000. Then an electrical fault in the boiler room triggered a calamitous fire on Easter Sunday, 1920. The writing had been on the wall during and after the First World War. Spa Days were already in free fall. The gravy train was stuck in the sidings. The fire marked the end of an era.

Nevertheless, Woodhall Spa continues to attract visitors. They come for the Kinema, the treelined avenues, the peace, the walks and the golf club. Woodhall is the headquarters of English Golf. The village also has a wonderful delicatessen where they bake their own bread and pies; a shoe shop claiming to be the smallest in Britain and innumerable cafés, including the *Ristorante in Parco*, an Italian brasserie attractively sited among the horse chestnuts and close to the Kinema. These establishments, apparently marooned in a sparsely-populated county, owe their continued success to a wealthy population of pensioners for whom Woodhall Spa is a sort of inland Eastbourne.

The architects of the Garden Village decreed that there should be no such thing as a street. The word had plebeian connotations. Consequently, you'll only find roads, avenues, courts and ways in Woodhall Spa. If you look closely, you'll also find four painted village signs on the four main approaches. Each sign is different and each tells a story. My favourite features colliery winding gear in the background while in the foreground, a cow drinks at a stream flowing from the pithead. All deeply significant.

The winding gear symbolises the first speculator who was drilling for coal when he hit water. The project was abandoned until a sick farmer's cow took a drink from the resulting stream and was miraculously cured. 'Forget about coal!' they chorused, 'Get the water!' That's how it all began.

Precisely where it went after that is recorded in the Cottage Museum where Marjorie's books are on sale. The cottage is fabulous – but then I have an affection for 'tin' buildings. The museum's an iron-clad prefab designed by the Norwich firm, Boulton and Paul which famously diversified into building aeroplanes. In 1887, it arrived at the station as a flatpack and became home to a certain Thomas and Mary Wield who made bathchairs to transport patients to and from the treatment rooms by donkey. With its wooden floors and tin walls, the Cottage Museum is its own best exhibit.

My mobile rang. It was the estate agent returning my call. He estimated that the Spa Baths had been intermittently on and off the market for 50 years. He told me the building was owned by a local family who want to sell. Banks Long & Co thought they were close to concluding a deal for half a million pounds in 2008, but it fell through. The price has now dropped to £200,000. There are, according to the agent, exciting opportunities to turn it into a hotel or back into a spa. Now that would be something. He said there were one or two interested parties. Then again, that's what they always say.

THERE'S SOMETHING IN THE WATER

Youlgrave, Derbyshire

In the Derbyshire Dales where men eat oatcakes for breakfast and play tug-of-war in the afternoon, there's a village called Youlgrave. Proud, independent, stubborn. So stubborn that when Severn Trent Water Board offered to help it out of a little local difficulty a few years ago, the village chorused: 'Naff off!'

This healthy disregard for authority is not uncommon in the Peak District. Youlgrave, however, is in a stronger position than most to hold up two metaphorical fingers. Since 1860 when Youlgrave Waterworks Ltd. came into being, the village has been more or less self-sufficient in this essential commodity. The kettles and bathtubs of a predominantly mining community were always filled from local supplies. Imagine the confidence, nay cockiness, that grows from such independence. Hosepipe bans? Fiddlesticks!

Then came a couple of bad droughts. Underground streams dried up. Youlgrave Waterworks Ltd. was in trouble. The company chairman, Harry Holland, told me things got so bad that the village had to *buy* water from Severn Trent. YWL was close to bankruptcy. The village would lose its virility as well as its H2O. Harry said:

'Severn Trent would have taken us over. We held an Extraordinary General Meeting and decided unanimously to maintain our independence whatever the cost. We'd enjoyed our own water for 140 years. We weren't inclined to stop!'

Youlgrave recovered from the glitch to consolidate its position as one of three communities in England which provide all their own water. It comes from beneath the sedimentary rocks and is processed at a small bunker in the corner of a field, otherwise known as Youlgrave Water Treatment Plant. From the outside it's Heath Robinson but the inside is an impressive collection of wires, pumps and gauges which cost several thousand pounds to install and do the job superbly well.

It's here that chlorine's added to the water, under the watchful gaze of three volunteers who keep the treatment works topped up every morning. I recall a local plumber, John Wardle, doing that job some years ago. He once boasted:

'Youlgrave water's like champagne. I can tell it from Severn Trent water blindfold. It's purer and sweeter. There's nowt like it.'

The Waterworks has an agreement with the Environment Agency that it won't extract more than 40 million gallons a year. That's easily enough to provide for 1,250 inhabitants and probably enough to supply surrounding villages too. Reopening Mawstone Mine made a huge difference. Immediately, an extra 20 million gallons came on-stream. It was a sensitive issue. Twelve young miners from the village were killed in a disaster at Mawstone in the 1930s. For the next seventy years, nobody wanted to go near the pithead, let alone plunder the underground reservoir. Eventually the pain subsided and the mine was reopened.

'I'll take you to the pithead,' said Harry.

We scrambled our way through the woods. He unlocked the grille over the main shaft. It hadn't been touched for two or three years. When Mawstone was reopened, men used the original winch to lower themselves into the mine from a different entrance. The silence and the blackness of the shaft gave no clue to the watery treasures which lay beneath. In order to access them, Youlgrave took a bank loan and put a couple of pence on the parish rate to repay it. Villagers thought it was a small price to pay for the privilege of their own supply.

In the village square, protected by iron railings, stands a circular stone fountain where women queued at six o'clock in the morning to fill their buckets. It took so long that they brought their knitting while the tap dribbled away. The fountain became a focal point for village gossip, as well as a marketplace for home-grown produce – the original parish pump.

Left: Miners' cottages add quaint character to this strong-minded Peak District village.

A plaque on the well reads:

The Fountain or Conduit Head. A reservoir of 1500 gallon capacity, erected in 1829 on the initiative of Youlgrave Friendly Society of Women to provide the village with its first piped water supply from a spring at Mawstone.

Just behind the pump is another extraordinary piece of Youlgrave, called Thimble Hall. It's the smallest detached house in the world, measuring 11 feet 10 inches by 10 feet 3 inches by 12 feet 2 inches high. There's no stairway. A ladder connects upstairs and down. Bruno Fredericks, a Chesterfield ice-cream baron, bought Thimble Hall in 1992, with plans to turn it into an ice-cream parlour. Then came the idea of a craft centre. When I dropped in again last November, it was still clamped in scaffolding. For now it remains a 'building at risk'.

John Wardle, the plumber has sadly passed away but before he died, I challenged him about his idle boast. Could he really distinguish Youlgrave water from the Severn Trent version? I presented him with two full glasses. He took a sip from the first and instantly declared it to be Youlgrave water. He didn't even try the second glass. He was, of course, spot on.

The 1500-gallon Conduit Head erected on the initiative of the Youlgrave Friendly Society of Women.

PHOTO CREDITS

Many photographers have provided their images of villages for this book. The author and the publisher wish to thank them all most warmly for their kind contributions.

Jacket	Normanton Church	**Paul Lemons**
13	Aldbrough	**David Flett**
13	Aldbrough	**Lee Hession**
10	Aldbrough	**John Blakeston**
18	Arnside	**Adrian Fretwell**
14	Arnside Viaduct	**Mark Fielding**
20	Avebury Manor	**Richard Bradshaw** www.flickr.com/photos/richard_bradshaw
20	Avebury Stone Circle	**Phil Selby**
19	Avebury Stone Circle	**Terje Hartberg**
22	Badby	**Tony Johns**
1	Badby Village	**Matthew Nobles**
25	Badby, Fawsley Hall	**Bob Hopkins**
26	Box Hill	**Keith Pharo**
28	Box Hill, cycle race	**Matthew Breach**
31	Brecklands, Afghan village	**Colonel Tony Powell, MoD**
35	Cerne Abbas Giant	**Kerry J Payne, NZ** (www.flickr.com/pjhotos/24462004@N07/)
32	Cerne Abbas Village	**Ken Hircock**
192	Chislehurst, Prickend Pond	**Donald Drage**
192	Chislehurst, Willett monument	**Adam Swaine**
38	Churchend derelict houses	**Lee Spalding**
37	Churchend, Foulness	**David Bullock**
42	Clovelly	**Chris Angula** (www.flickr.com/photos/outinthesticks)
44	Clovelly harbour	**Chris Angula** (www.flickr.com/photos/outinthesticks)
45	Clovelly Lobster Festival	**Clovelly Estate**
45	Clovelly lobsters	**Clovelly Estate**
50	Craster, Robson's kippers	**Adrian Fretwell**
46	Craster Village	**Callum Stewart**
49	Craster, Dunstanburgh Castle	**Mike Smith**
53	Downham	**Marian Byrne**
57	Drax Power Station	**Alan Green**
54	Drax Power Station	**Sean Robinson**
59	Dungeness	**Karen Roe**
2	Dungeness	**Richard Watkins**
62	Dungeness Power Station	**www.jeremysage.co.uk**
65	East Bergholt, Lott's House	**Colin & Louise English**
66	East Bergholt, Flatford Mill	**Roger Cave**
68-9	Eel Pie Island	**Kevin Grosvenor** (www.flickr.com/photos/loopingstar)
71, 72, 73	Eel Pie Island	**Fabienne Henry** (author of the blog lostinlondon.fr)
78	Elan miner	**Steve Bevan**
75	Elan valley (Craig Goch)	**Yvonne Courtine**
76-7	Elan village	**Linda Westlake**
80	Eyam	**David Pursglove**
83	Eyam Hall	**Richad Paxman**
86	Eyam plague cottages	**Kevin Reilly**
88	Flash village	**Gary Sheldon**
174	Froncysyllte	**Shaun Jones**
170	Froncysyllte aqueduct	**Robert Silverwood**
17	Froncysyllte village	**Stuart Cook** (www.flickr.com/photos/10126769@N05)
3	Grantchester water meadows	**Ann Miles** (www.pin-sharp.co.uk)
94	Grantchester, Mill House	**Ann Miles** (www.pin-sharp.co.uk)
92	Grantchester, Ruper Brooke statue	**Paul Rudkin**
96	Great Tew	**Andrew Dennes**
100	Hallaton	**Norm Horner**
101, 102	Hallaton	**Duncan Ellson**

Photo Credits

Particular thanks to Adrian Fretwell, nine of whose photographs are published here: pages 50, 113, 158, 167, 182, 183, 190, 193, 195